VOID

One World, Many Families

Edited by

Karen Altergott, Ph.D.

Published by

National Council on Family Relations
Minneapolis, MN

NCFR

In observance of
The United Nations 1994 International
Year of the Family

The National Council on Family Relations was established in 1938 as a multi-disciplinary professional association to provide a forum for family researchers, educators, and practitioners to share in the development and dissemination of knowledge about families and family relationships, to establish professional standards, and to promote family policies that enhance their well-being. NCFR is privately supported through its members and sale of publications and educational programs. Beneficiaries of NCFR services include family professionals, policy makers and educators.

The United Nations General Assembly in resolution 44/82 of December 8, 1989, proclaimed 1994 as the International Year of the Family with the theme: "Family: Resources and Responsibilities in a Changing World."

ISBN-0-916174-38-7

Cover Design: Thomas Cassidy

National Council on Family Relations
3989 Central Avenue NE, Suite 550
Minneapolis, MN 55421
612-781-9331
FAX 612-781-9348

Preface

by Karen Altergott, Ph.D.

In April, 1991, volunteers from a variety of NCFR Sections formed a planning committee for the 1994 U.N. International Year of the Family. The group considered ways NCFR could acknowledge, celebrate and contribute to this global event. This collection of essays is one result of the committee's work. In this volume, we join in the international process of understanding and improving family life. The essays presented here are intended to stimulate discussion about the issues families face all around the globe. They do not provide definitive answers.

Each essay represents a call for your attention and a call to further work. I hope these essays will lead to greater awareness of and involvement with the many and diverse families that comprise our world. The themes of the U.N. International Year of the Family are presented first. Several authors then provide ideas about the interface between national policy and the condition of families and the use of policies to enhance family life. Next, a set of essays on the variations in resources, the dependencies of children, the gendered realities of adult family roles, divorce as a family experience, and aging in the multigenerational family systems analyze shared concerns about the family life course. Essays on race and ethnicity, on religion, and on family education for peace provide illustrations of family strengths under challenge. Essays on refugees and violence illustrate the challenges faced daily by millions of families and the new strengths and supports required. Summarizing these essays and directing our vision toward further action, the final essay links this work to the future.

Many individuals contributed ideas, efforts and time to this project. The initial planning group included Richard Gelles, M. Janice Hogan, Judy Myers-Walls, Lynda Walters, Connie Steele, Connie Shehan, and me. Mary Jo Czaplewski often sustained the energy and provided continuity through all phases of this effort. While I began my involvement by proposing a publication, the NCFR effort rapidly expanded into several components. In addition to this publication, an international health policy forum, several publications, and a workshop are all products of NCFR's work on the U.N. International Year of the Family. Barbara Elliott, M. Janice Hogan and Lynda Walters stepped into leadership roles when it became clear that the NCFR-IYF agenda was expanding. Gary Lee, Brent Miller and Stephen Jorgensen provided counsel as part of their leadership roles. Many others over the past two years have participated in various meetings, telephone conversations and have lent their support to the effort.

In addition to the authors, reviewers contributed to the strength and quality of this volume. Reviewers included Barbara Elliott, Lina Fong, M. Janice Hogan, Dean Knudsen, Judy Myers-Walls, Connie Shehan, and Lynda Walters. The task of completing the volume was facilitated by the staff at the NCFR office, who dialogued regarding appropriate artwork for the cover, who enabled last minute corrections, and who were resourceful and efficient in all their efforts.

Many people supported this project in particular ways. Most importantly, though, is the general support of the NCFR membership for new thinking about the many families of our one world. Our way of thinking is open to the world, and the international perspective is now well-woven throughout NCFR's mission. This is expressed through our rapidly expanding international network of colleagues, in our educational innovations and in the concern for correct action in the research, education, practice and policy arenas.

One World, Many Families

The International Year of the Family: The World's Support for the Smallest Democracy

Henryk J. Sokalski

Henryk J. Sokalski
United Nations
Coordinator for the
International Year of the Family
Vienna, Austria

"We are at a crossroads between what the family was in the past, what it is now and what it will and should be in the future."

Every family, in its own way, is an unexplored mystery. It has been so since the very emergence of humankind's oldest social institution, compounded as it was by the growing diversity of its forms, concepts and definitions. Yet, the concept of the family is perhaps the most basic one in social life. Families are a universal phenomenon. Almost all individuals are members of a family during their lifetime. Their entire life is affected by what the family managed to invest in them or failed to provide in terms of the natural environment for their growth and well-being. Vital, productive families are essential to the world's future; they are the cradle of the generations to come. Their strengths and weaknesses largely reflect the societal fabric of every country.

As the world's oldest form of human relationship, the family has survived thousands of years, withstanding odds of the highest order. But it has not remained untouched by social change. In fact, there has been a dramatic transformation in the perception of the family. Consequently, we are at a crossroads between what the family was in the past, what it is now and what it will and should be in the future.

The family is a living social institution affected by socioeconomic factors. Notwithstanding a general consensus that family is a basic unit of society, perhaps the most universally applicable statement about the family is that it is diverse and dynamic. There is no simple view of the family, nor is there a comprehensive and universally applicable definition. Furthermore, perceptions of the functions and roles of the family and notions of the ideal interpersonal relationships within the family may differ both among and within national societies, religions and cultures. In addition to this existing diversity, new and divergent family forms and functions continue to evolve in different societies.

Because of their universal and historical importance, families as social, economic and cultural forms have been taken for granted for too long. And their strengths and resilience are sorely tested by policies and programs which do not reflect the realities of family life. Similarly, there is a prevalent expectation that families have the capacity to adapt to new and very demanding challenges. Under the brutal pressures of economic recession, structural adjustment and massive social change, many governments are retreating from a central social policy role as service-provider. Families seem to be the principal social safety net to absorb this caring responsibility. In many Western industrialized countries, the welfare state faltered. In Eastern and Central European countries, unsuccessful economies and political systems are in transition. And, in developing countries, where family and kinship constituted the basis of social support for the majority of population, the processes of industrialization, modernization and urbanization have contributed to the erosion of traditional family values of mutual support, thus placing increasing demands on social welfare systems that are already under severe pressures of various kinds.

An evolution has also been taking place in the sphere of relationships within societies. All over the world, there has been an unusual upsurge of democratic aspirations towards more popular participation, pluralism, transparency and accountability of government - towards a civil society. For this positive process to develop, and win, individuals need to be better equipped to counteract the challenges of the obsolete. Societies can become democratic if the families they comprise are based on democratic principles. Life in a repressive family, which has no respect for the rights of the individual, can be an experience even harsher than functioning in a repressive society. They are both unacceptable.

The conviction that policies supporting families are of paramount significance in the present-day socioeconomic context transcends political ideologies in almost every country of the world. As the 1970s and 1980s witnessed an ever increasing concern for the well-being and fundamental rights of the individual, particularly those of the disadvantaged, marginalized or discriminated against, efforts to improve their lot concurrently led to the "re-discovery" of the family. An important corollary of those activities has been the recognition of the family as a crucial social network for improving the well-being of individuals and as a major resource base for development and social progress. From this revitalized concern for the situation of families and their role in social policy and development emerged a growing conviction that concrete measures supporting families and increased international cooperation on family issues was urgently needed. The United Nations General Assembly responded with the proclamation of 1994 as the International Year of the Family (IYF), with its pragmatic theme: *"Family: resources and responsibilities in a changing world."*

The proclamation of the Year and its preparatory process so far have clearly revealed that one common difficulty. The lack of a clear understanding of what families are has plagued the efforts of governments to deal with families in social policy. Despite the fact that governments are turning to families for solutions, there is a significant lack of accurate information on families. In short, there is much about them that we do not know.

What is often claimed to be known about families by those who influence families is founded on intuition, anecdote and experience. We need a rigorous and systematically constructed understanding of what families are in order to develop programs and policies. Nor is it clear that existing legal and policy frameworks regarding families reflect the contemporary realities of family life. Therefore, when seen in the context of an increasing social policy reliance on families, fostering the rediscovery of the family through improving our knowledge is clearly an important objective of the International Year of the Family.

Despite deficient information and critical need for current research, I am far from suggesting that we know nothing about families. On the contrary, there is a significant body of literature and knowledge which can and must be brought before legislators and policy-makers to inform and provoke constructive action. This knowledge, in combination with informed debate at all levels concerning the International Year of the Family, has greatly contributed to arriving at a general international consensus regarding at least five major issues which guide the process of IYF preparations:

- **First**, that the family is the natural and fundamental group unit of society and is entitled to protection by society and the State.
- **Second**, that there exist various concepts of the family in different social, cultural and political systems.
- **Third**, that respect for human rights, particularly gender equality, women's equal participation in employment and shared familial responsibilities are essential elements of modern family policy.
- **Fourth**, that families are the fullest reflection, at the grass-roots level, of the strengths and weaknesses of the social and developmental welfare environment and, as such, offer a uniquely comprehensive and amalgamating approach to social issues.
- **Fifth**, that families, as basic units of social life, are major agents of sustainable development at all levels of society, and their contribution to that process is crucial for its success.

Against the backdrop of those unifying International Year of the Family guide-posts, which reveal an essential unity in diversity of family life all over the world, there is a host of problems, which one can hardly disregard, during and after 1994.

With economic development and the spread of new forms of economic activity, family-based subsistence labor has been replaced by work for wages, specialization of labor and concentration of activities in a workplace which is removed from the home. While urbanization has brought the comforts of modern life as well as access to services and job opportunities, it has also changed human relations, making them more instrumental. Masses of people have migrated from rural areas into cities in the hope of gaining a share of the benefits of urban development, only to find themselves sharing the misery of slums.

The recent socio-political transitions in many countries have placed millions of families in totally alien situations, left to themselves without support to survive under the mechanisms of market economies. Recent and ongoing wars in different regions force families out of their homes and countries. The current number of refugee families is unprecedented in history. Particularly in parts of Africa, prolonged and recurrent devastation of nature exacerbated by war and serious economic decline has led to the disintegration of families. Families and individuals are caught in a vicious circle of starvation and disease. With severe fiscal pressures, social services are cut back, reducing the safety net for the population at the very time when it is most needed. Female-headed single-parent families, in particular, tend to be economically vulnerable, as the female wage-earner often works for inequitably low wages. Many families find the constant need to balance work and familial responsibilities to be among the most demanding aspects of daily life. Greater numbers of people in urban and rural areas are becoming aware of opportunities for alternative life-styles. Institutional education, early maturation of children, their ability to earn incomes independently of the family and the development of a youth culture have all lessened the influence of the family in the process of socialization in late childhood and early adulthood. When children drop out of school early and the family is limited in performing its socialization function, children can develop antisocial behaviors or turn to drugs as an avenue for recognition, escape or gratification. Adequate social mechanisms to provide solutions to these and other problems have yet to be developed.

The forces of change have not spared relationships within families either. Foremost among them, particularly in the industrialized world, are the sweeping accomplishments by and on behalf of women. The father as breadwinner is no longer the norm, and the middle-class family can no longer meet its increasing needs through a single income. Not only have increasing numbers of women entered the labor force, which was once the preserve of men, but they are remaining there following marriage. They also enjoy greater access to education and vocational training. Demographic analyses point to a very clear correlation between women's educational level and the kind of paid employment they obtain, the age at which they marry, their age at the birth of their first child and the number and health of their children. Despite these accomplishments, many women in the world suffer under repressive patriarchal models of family life.

The structural changes in the family have created problems for many men in their identities as husbands and fathers, at least in the Western world. The undermined importance of the breadwinner role for men has meant, unfortunately, that more fathers are negligent of their responsibilities. From the point of view of social policy or legislative change, the challenge is to ensure that the financial responsibilities of fathers are recognized without strengthening the view that financial support is the only familial role and exclusive province of fatherhood. Likewise, families must not be penalized for attempting to have fathers assume more nurturing and active childrearing roles or assume an equitable responsibility for domestic work.

Governmental responses to family issues are numerous. They are increasingly based on international standards, notably the *International Covenants on Human Rights*, the *United Nations Convention on the Elimination of All Forms of Discrimination Against Women*, and the *Convention on the Rights of the Child*. A simple illustrative example is that, in response to the new forms and structures of families, steps have been taken in many countries to ensure that relevant national laws and administrative procedures reflect the reality of diverse forms of families. Other major areas of attention have included: measures to ensure supportive networks in the fulfillment of caring functions of families, such as through child care facilities; measures to enable couples and parents to reconcile family and work responsibilities, such as income security and provisions for maternal leave, paternal leave and flexible working hours; measures to promote gender equality and the situation of women, such as labor force participation, equal rights in divorce and matrimonial property, and reduction of domestic violence; measures to promote maternal and child health; measures to promote the well-being and rights of the child, including reducing child poverty, combatting malnutrition, providing compulsory education and socialization, addressing child abuse and neglect in the family. Interesting specific measures in this regard are the development of a child-centered family policy, e.g. removal of parent from the family in cases of abuse rather than the child, the creation of an ombudsman for children; and family support measures, including through taxation policy.

The world community, be it at the governmental or nongovernmental level, seems to be cognizant that the International Year of the Family is not an end in itself. It is rather a beginning of a long process, which has started with the Year's proclamation. It is a unique opportunity to cast a new mold for world events of this type, bringing into play the various national bodies that ultimately have the most immediate impact on the situation of individuals and families. In pursuing its objectives, one has to be selective, consistent and, indeed, farsighted. Having stressed the major emphasis of the Year on national and local levels, its program identifies three specific issues as a starting point for an identification of priorities:

- **Issue one:** strengthening family's ability to meet its own needs.
- **Issue two:** clarifying and understanding the balance between how the family can satisfy its needs and what it can expect through public provision of services.
- **Issue three:** recognizing the effects of societal ills on and in family relationships and acknowledging that government policy intervention may be needed to counter negative behavior or exploitation in the family.

IYF preparations have forcefully revealed the need for relationships in the family to be based upon principles defined as *democratic* in societies. Whenever asked whether the family can be democratic, I say I think it can; I think it should; and I believe it will be democratic, one day. Actually, the future of the family as a social institution may hinge on its democratization. Hence, the motto of our International Year of the Family: "***Building the Smallest Democracy at the Heart of Society***".

The ancient concept of natural law finds its most visible expression in the concept of individual human rights. Inalienable human rights, in a fully developed concept of democracy, is the anchor which defines and limits the obligations and relationships of the individual to the community, State and society. Such rights circumscribe the compromises an individual may make, or the State can expect, for the benefit of the greater community. Families as social groups are not exempt from the obligation to recognize and respect the basic human rights of their members.

It is not, however, a requirement that democracy in the family should neutralize its ability to direct the actions of its members, sanction negative behavior or be a source of social control. As the most immediate social environment for individuals, a family with democratic obligations is the first group to be entrusted with the responsibility to protect the rights of its members, particularly those in a position of vulnerability. When a family rests at, or descends to, the point where the basic human rights of individual members are endangered by others within the unit, the costs to the greater society and the individuals involved cannot be measured in any currency.

More than anything else, building the smallest democracy implies that the process of familial problem-solving is facilitated and enhanced through mechanisms that permit the interests of family members to be represented where the rights of dependent or vulnerable members are respected, and redress for injustices exists both within and outside the family unit. In families, as in nation States, the capacity to survive as a functioning stable unit depends largely on their ability to manage conflict, solve problems, repair discord and channel opposing views into a constructive agenda for action. This is fundamental to the survival of democracies and is equally indispensable to individual families. By shifting the locus of action and the associated resources to the level of families, we create a society which is much more well-prepared to meet the diverse challenges that herald the new millennium, by introducing a level of problem-solving flexibility not present in most of our existing support services.

International years under the aegis of the United Nations have had both their enthusiasts and skeptics. The latter have usually been those who expected too much from such *short-term observances*; they seem not to realize that the main purpose of those events is first and foremost awareness-raising of problems involved and preparing ground for *long-term action*. I wish to assure all those who might still be skeptical about the IYF that much progress has been made throughout its preparatory process to enhance effective work in those two areas. May it also be stressed that:

1) the International Year of the Family will not result in an attempt to impose a standard definition of the family or promote a specific family model;
2) the International Year of the Family will not weaken the national and international accomplishments in the struggle for the rights of the child or the enjoyment of equal rights by women and men since the objectives of IYF and of the advancement of women must be pursued in complete synergy; and,
3) **the observances of IYF will promote a balanced perspective of families based on an appreciation of both rights and responsibilities.**

Families will continue to evolve, perhaps in unpredictable ways. The challenge is to ensure that policy also evolves accordingly and remains both relevant and effective. The success of the International Year of the Family and its follow-up will ultimately have to be measured in terms of meeting this task.

Families in Transition: America's and the World's

Arlene Skolnick

Arlene Skolnick, Ph.D.
Professor, Institute of Human
Development
University of California
Berkeley

"In the context of social change, families ... display remarkable adaptability, resilience & inherent strength ... To [further] strengthen families, the combined effort of researchers, policy makers & families themselves is needed."

United Nations Occasional Papers Series, No. 2, 1992. "Family: Forms and Functions", pg. 17.

Over the past three decades, family life in the industrialized nations changed dramatically. The trends are remarkably similar across North America and Western Europe—later marriage, falling fertility rates, more divorce, single parent families, increasing numbers of women working outside the home, increasing diversity of family forms. Indeed, there is also increasing uncertainty about how to define the family.

To be sure, countries differ in current and past rates of various demographic indicators. The United States has higher divorce rates than most other countries; Sweden has higher rates of unmarried cohabitation. But regardless of national variations, the broad dimensions of family change are similar across the Western world and even beyond. It does not seem too farfetched to suggest that we are witnessing another world revolution in family patterns (Goode, 1963).

Although everyone agrees that a profound transformation has occurred, there is no consensus as to what it means. Is the family becoming an endangered species? Have family bonds lost their value? While family scholars debate whether or not the family is in decline, many people, particularly in the United States, take the disintegration of the family to be a simple social fact. Family issues have been a major battleground in American politics.

How do we make sense of these striking transformations? In this paper, I argue that recent family trends must be understood as responses to long-term societal change. The twentieth century has witnessed major economic, demographic, social, and political transformations, and these have set the stage for major shifts in family life. The trends are most pronounced in the industrialized world, but reflect global forces. Each country's response to family change, however, is shaped by its own cultural and political traditions.

State of Present Knowledge

The question "What happened to the family?" is often answered with vague, usually disapproving references to feminism, "the sixties", or increasing hedonism and individualism. Yet family change and value shifts do not occur in a societal vacuum. In fact, the family has always been in flux. At periods of societal transition, change is especially rapid and dislocating.

Briefly, three distinct but related structural shifts seem to have set the current cycle of family change in motion: first, the move towards a "post-industrial" service and information economy; second, reductions in mortality and fertility that reshaped the individual and family life course; and third, a psychological transformation rooted mainly in rising educational levels (Skolnick, 1991).

The shift to post-industrial economy undid the breadwinner/housewife family pattern widely seen as traditional. Historically, however, that family arrangement is an "aberration" that emerges in the early stages of industrialization, and tends to recur in countries now undergoing development (Davis, 1988). It declines as service jobs increase, drawing women into the paid labor force. Other countries are in different stages of the same process; for example, in Japan, while the majority of wives are still unpaid family workers, a rapidly increasing number are moving into the workplace. In many Middle Eastern countries, there is a tension between the desire to keep women at home and the need for workers to do the kind of service work women do in the West.

The demographic transformations over the last century are no less dramatic than the economic. Two thirds of the total increase in longevity since prehistoric times has taken place since 1900 (Preston, 1976). Before the turn of century, only 40% of women lived through all the stages of a "normal" life course--growing up, marrying, having children, and surviving with a spouse to the age of 50 (Uhlenberg, 1980). Half of all parents experienced the death of a child, a quarter of all children lost a parent. The rates of family disruption by death were almost as high as the rate of disruption by divorce today.

As life spans lengthened and fertility declined, the portrait of the nuclear family as parents and young children came to describe only a small segment of the life course. For women, raising children is no longer an occupation that fills most of life. Most of the parent-child relationship takes place when both parties are adults. The "empty nest" period is a stage of married life that did not exist in earlier centuries.

The third major transformation is a set of psycho-cultural changes that might be described as "psychological gentrification" (Skolnick, 1991). That is, cultural advantages once enjoyed only by the upper classes, such as higher education, spread to those lower in the social hierarchy. Psychological gentrification also involves increased leisure, travel, and exposure to information, as well as a general rise in the standard of living. Despite the persistence of poverty, unemployment, and economic insecurity in the industrialized world, less of the population than in the historical past is living at the level of sheer subsistence.

Throughout Western society, rising levels of education and related changes have been linked to a complex set of shifts in personal and political attitudes. One of these is a psychological approach to life—greater introspectiveness, a yearning for warmth and intimacy in family and other relationships, (Veroff, Douvan, & Kulka, 1981). There is also evidence of a widespread shift towards a more companionate ideal of marriage, and a more democratic family. Instead of obedience, Western parents have increasingly come to desire independence and autonomy in their children (Alwin, 1988). More broadly, these changes in attitude have been described as a shift to "postmaterialist values" emphasizing self-expression, tolerance, equality, a concern for the quality of life (Inglehart, 1990).

These historic shifts have brought both costs and benefits: family relations have become more fragile and more emotionally rich, mass longevity has brought us a host of problems as well as the gift of extended life. Change has brought greater opportunities for women, but because of persisting gender inequality, women have borne a large share of the costs. But we cannot turn the clock back to the family models of the past. Further, despite nostalgia for the "world we have lost", few of us would actually want to return to conditions of life endured by most people in generations past.

Implications of Change

Paradoxically, after all the upheavals of the recent decades, the emotional and cultural significance of the family persists. Family remains the center of most people's lives, and as numerous surveys show, a cherished value. While marriage has become more fragile, the parent-child relationship—especially the mother-child relationship—remains a core attachment across the life course (Rossi & Rossi, 1990).

The family, however, can be both "here to stay" and beset with difficulties. There is widespread recognition that the massive social and economic changes we have lived through call for public and private sector policies in support of families. Most European countries have recognized for some time that governments have a role in supplying an array of supports to families—health care, children's allowances, housing subsidies, support for working parents and children, such as child care, parental leave, shorter work days for parents, as well as an array of services for older persons.

Each country's response to these changes, as we've noted earlier, has been shaped by its own political and cultural traditions. Because of their historical similarities, comparisons between the United States and Canada are particularly revealing. While the U.S. remains embroiled in a cultural war over the family, Canada has been making quiet adaptations to recent family trends.

Although Canada lacks the kind of comprehensive family policies found in Northern Europe, it is in many ways a "kinder, gentler" country than the U.S. (Dreier & Bernard, 1993). Canada has less poverty, lower infant mortality rates, and lower teenage pregnancy rates. In large part, these differences are due to a stronger social safety net: paid maternity leave, annual cash payments to all families with children (reclaimed through taxes from higher income families), a child tax credit, as well as direct cash assistance to low income families. Canada also enjoys universal health insurance and old age pensions. A similar safety net sustains families in Australia, a sister country to the U.S. and Canada. As a result of these policies, these countries have been spared much of the poverty and social disintegration that has plagued the United States in the last decade (Edgar, 1993; Smeeding, 1992).

Both Canada and the U.S. are marked by regional, racial, and ethnic divisions. But in contrast to the U.S. "melting pot" ideal, Canadians have traditionally seen their country as a "mosaic" in which cultural differences are recognized and even encouraged. Perhaps because of this heritage of cultural pluralism, Canada has had less difficulty assimilating recent changes in the family.

Canada has also been more accepting of changes in women's roles and status. In 1982 it incorporated an equal rights amendment into its constitution, and feminist issues are discussed at all levels of the government (Begin, 1988). In the United States, by contrast, a powerful backlash developed in response to the women's movement and the social changes of the 1970s. Americans still argue, for example, whether mothers should work outside the home, and whether other changes of recent years can somehow be reversed. In the early 1990s, however, an increasing number of social scientists and corporate executives have begun to call for the United States to meet the challenges of a post-industrial era by developing public and private policies in support of families.

Looking Ahead

The world at the end of the twentieth century is vastly different from what it was at the beginning, or even in the middle. Families are struggling to adapt to new realities. The countries that have been at the leading edge of family change still find themselves caught midway between yesterday's norms, today's new realities, and an uncertain future.

As we have seen, changes in women's lives have been a pivotal factor in recent family trends. In many countries there is a considerable gap between men's and women's attitudes and expectations of one another. Even where both partners accept a more equal division of labor in the home, there is often a gap between attitudes and behavior. In no country have employers, the government, or men fully caught up to the changes in women's lives.

The ferment in women's roles is now global, prompted not just by education and economic development, but women's participation in independence and other grass roots movements. The United Nations has legitimized the global discussion of women's lives and rights, through a number of world conferences on women, as well as the vision of the family articulated for the Year of the Family: "The Smallest

Democracy at the Heart of the Society".

Family patterns, however, do not necessarily change quickly, nor in the same direction. Tradition can and does coexist with modernity. Indeed, a forceful reassertion of patriarchy is a feature of various fundamentalisms around the world. In Eastern Europe, the collapse of Communist regimes has led to a resurgence of "traditional" notions of women's roles. Diversity is likely to be a continuing feature of family life, not just because of traditional differences in terms of race, class, and ethnicity, but because so many family matters are now based on individual choice.

To be effective, government policies must recognize the pluralism of family forms, as well as diversity within families. The needs of individuals and families vary across the life course; infancy and early childhood, adolescence, and old age pose particular challenges in modern societies that need to be addressed. More broadly, the interests and perspectives of different family members do not always coincide. A focus on "family" should never obscure the fact that "his" marriage is not necessarily the same as "hers", or that the parents' family is not necessarily the child's.

The family around the world is likely to be "in transition" well into the 21st century. Anthropological and historical studies of cultural change suggest that is a long and often painful process (Wallace, 1970), marked by individual and family stress, and political and cultural conflict. There are no quick, inexpensive solutions to solving the problems besetting family life today. Yet any government in an advanced industrial society that ignores the well-being of its children and families does so at its peril.

References

Alwin, D. F. (1988). From obedience to autonomy: Changes in traits desired in children, 1924-1978. Public Opinion Quarterly, 52, pp. 33-52.

Begin, M. Debates and silences: Reflections of a politician in search of Canada. Fall Issue of Daedalus, 117:335-362.

Dreier, P., & Bernard, E. (1993, Winter). Kinder, gentler Canada. The American Prospect, 12:85-88.

Edgar, D. Families in the 1990's: A challenge for future policy approaches. Paper prepared for the Social Policy Directorate. Melbourne: Australian Institute of Family Studies.

Goode, W. J. (1963). World revolution and family patterns. New York: Free Press.

Inglehart, R. (1990). Culture Shift. New Jersey: Princeton University Press.

Preston, S. J. (1976). Mortality patterns in national populations: With special references to recorded courses of death. New York: Academic Press.

Rossi, A. S., & Rossi, P. H. (1990). Of human bonding: Parent-child relations across the life course. Hawthorne, NY: Aldine de Gruyter.

Skolnick, A. (1991). Embattled paradise: The American family in an age of uncertainty. New York: Basic Books.

Smeeding, T. M. (1993, January-February). Why the U.S. antipoverty system doesn't work very well. Challenge, pp. 30-35.

Uhlenberg, P. (1980). Death and the family. Journal of Family History, 5(3), 313-320.

Veroff, Douvan, & Kulka, (1981). The inner America: A self portrait from 1957-1976. New York: Basic Books.

Wallace, A. F. C. (1970). The death and rebirth of the Seneca. New York: Knopf.

Note: *Based on "The Situation of Families in North America", a consultant paper presented at the United Nations Europe and North America Preparatory Meeting for the International Year of the Family, Valetta, Malta, April 26-30, 1993.*

Nations and States
Enacting Policy for Families

Shirley Baugher

Shirley Baugher, Ph.D.
Chair, Family and Consumer
Sciences
University of Nebraska-Lincoln

"Social policy must seek to overcome... limited perceptions if the human condition is to improve, the eradication of poverty is to be a realistic goal and society is to be based upon the principle of distributive justice."

United Nations Occasional Papers Series, No. 1, 1992. *Family Matters*, pg. 25.

Nations and states establish regulations, policies, and structures that impact families. How these are designed, implemented, and evaluated depends on belief systems about the value of the family within society; about individual vs. group or corporate rights; and about the role of public authority in guiding and influencing family life. Recommendations regarding family policies must be sensitive to diverse cultures and political beliefs to avoid negative consequences for families.

State of Present Knowledge

The basic principles that support the International Year of the Family, as established by the United Nations, are those of the Universal Bill of Human Rights. One principle states that the family is the basic unit of society; as such the family must be accorded the protection and assistance to assure that it can assume responsibility within the community (pursuant to the provisions of the Universal Declaration of Human Rights, article 16.3). Therefore, it is reasonable to conclude that the expectations of family policies are basic to human rights.

Questions similar to those experienced in a dialogue about universal human rights emerge in a dialogue about family policy. Students of human rights often ask, "Is it appropriate to expect universal human rights within and between diverse cultures?" Students of family policy might ask the same question. Societal values regarding the functions and roles of the family differ both among and within countries. Studies of family issues and policies in various countries and cultures generate an understanding that a dialogue about family policy is certainly culture-specific and probably country-specific.

Similarly, views on the extent to which the community or government should intervene and influence the decisions made in families also vary according to differing interpretations of what is good for society. What is the right or responsibility of institutions (public or private) to make decisions about individual or groups rights?

An initial understanding about the "philosophy of rights" may be gained by examining political philosophies of nations and states. Forsythe, in <u>Human Rights and World Politics</u>, outlined three political philosophies and the beliefs about rights within each (a continuum within each is reflected in the examples on the table below). Conservatism states that only the strongest and the most powerful have rights...eliminating the weak. Liberalism defines a central belief that the highest good or value is individual well-being and that personal well-being is found through freedom and equality. Communalism states that rights stem from membership in a community or group. Individuals form solid groups and it is the group that governs their rights.

Table 1: POLITICAL PHILOSOPHIES AND HUMAN RIGHTS			
Label	**Communalism**	**Liberalism**	**Conservatism**
Rhetoric	right of worker class or national group to equality	right to equal freedom and material equality for individuals	unequal rights or rights for the most powerful
Example	China Algeria	Sweden USA	Brazil Paraguay

As nations and states operate within a political philosophy, there are great differences of attitudes about human rights. The attitude about family differs within each political philosophic practice; it is important to understand the basic beliefs about the role of the family within the culture to understand the motivation for the development of family policies. The political philosophy also provides the framework for beliefs concerning the role of the State in the family.

In a political culture that practices rights for the most powerful, for example, we witness the mass murder of street children. In the communal political culture of China, child care is subsidized with the intent to provide social learning opportunities for "only children" (a result of the population control policy). Subsidized child care in Mexico exists because of the growing number of women in the labor force without the traditional support of family to provide care for children.

The current debate in the United States about the placement of children in "foster care" provides an example of the practices that evolve from philosophic beliefs about individual vs. family value within society. If the individual is perceived to be more important than the family, then placing children outside of the home is an acceptable process and policy for the protection of children's rights. If the family is perceived to be the primary nurturer of children, then support of the family to insure the well-being of children is a more acceptable process and policy to protect children.

Exemplary Action on Behalf of Families

Western Europe has a long history of responsiveness to the issues of family policy. Family policy is considered to be a part of social policy, a much better defined and more self-conscious field. European family policy has been conventionally pro-natalist, encouraging population growth by supporting larger families with some form of social wage. While there are diversified values in Europe, there is a mobilized political constituency that agrees on an ultimate goal-to provide support for children and their families. An examination of the major components of an European Family policy agenda reveals income transfers for children and their families; child and family allowances; maternity and parenting insurance benefits; guaranteed minimum child support payments; free, voluntary preschool education; family related employment leave policies; and national health service programs.

Latin and South American populations exhibit familism, proposed as one of the most important specific values of their cultures. Individuals have a strong identification with and attachment to their family. These are characterized by loyalty, reciprocity and solidarity among members of the family. Through an extensive extended family network, that has historically remained intact, the work of the family is well defined.

In recent years, the family in Latin and South America has experienced change, due to the changing economy, migration and increased labor participation by women. Mexico is an example of this transition. Many families can no longer support nannies in the home to care for children and extended families are no longer intact to care for children. The official role of the wife of the President of Mexico is to direct the "Desarrollo Integral para la Familia" (DIF), primarily concerned with the welfare of children. The recent focus of this system of professionals has been the establishment of "guarderias", or child care centers, for children.

The family in China has been in transition for decades; perhaps the most internationally well known family policy in China is the "one child per family" rule. However, China has established an extensive network of child care centers to support the development and socialization of many "only children". Child development programs focus on activities that allow children to learn and work in competitive and cooperative ways....through the expression of physical exercise, art, music, storytelling, and sharing meals.

In the United States, California experimented with the development of a comprehensive family policy agenda in the 1980s. What is significant about the initial work of the legislative task force was that the diverse constituents across the state could not agree on what constituted a family. Finally, the task force agreed to write an agenda based on the <u>functions</u> of the family to avoid a dialogue about "the right kind of family". The task force developed a package of 46 bills that were divided into 10 categories (with specific goals in each); the categories included housing, health care, jobs/wages, dependent care, child care, programs for adolescents, adult and eldercare, family/school relationships, parent education and support, and human service delivery.

An examination of the motives for existing family policies, regardless of the nation or state, reveals several themes. Those are pro-natalism, labor market policy (generally linked to the number of women in the labor force), income redistribution, the cost of child care, and gender equity.

The themes are expressed through numerous policies; family leave and flextime are two practices that address labor market and child care issues. Flexible scheduling was first developed in the late 1960s in Germany, with the intention of reducing travel to and from work. Flextime spread to other countries, especially Britain. Foreign industries with the most flexible workplace policies are those disproportionately staffed by women.

At least 122 countries world-wide have paid family leave. This includes all of Europe, most of Africa, Asia, the Middle East, Canada, and Latin America. Almost every country with a family leave law combines both job protection and some wage replacement, key components of paid family leave, for at least part of the leave. Pregnancy and early infant care leave includes pre-birth time through time to care for the child in early stages of infancy. Sweden allows parents to take a total of 48 weeks off; Australia allows women to take up to 52 weeks of unpaid maternity leave. France provides extended child care leave and allows workers to take up to 2 years off, with partial wages. Sick family care leave allows for workers to care for a sick parent, child, spouse, or household member. Canada permits up to 12 weeks family care leave.

If a nation or state develops policy to address the functions of the family in the context of these themes, there may be an opportunity to develop "a universal concept of family policy". The specific programs and practices to support families will vary according to the political philosophy of the nation and the belief about the role of family within society.

Looking Ahead

Dizard and Gadlin, in <u>The Minimal Family</u>, stated that the modern family is indeed a number of families. The specific form a given family takes is a function of what the individuals bring to the relationship-convictions, ethnic traditions and personal desire. This is not a new concept. DeTocqueville defined the family as a principle of conduct and a substitute for the bureaucracies and public policies that now influence virtually every aspect of individual and family life (in the West).

Each nation or state must address its basic assumptions about family and the role of healthy families in its society. Do we believe the family to be at the heart of a healthy functioning society? Do we believe that intact families are critical to the well being of children and therefore the future well-being of society? Do we believe that families provide the basic environment that develops the capacity to learn and therefore contribute to an educated society? Do we believe the role of government to be that of supporting families in discharging their functions or do we believe that government should provide substitutes for such functions? Is there a political constituency that can agree on basic values and goals for families and develop a consensus for the future? Is there a political constituency that can establish goals for the development of policies that will impact families?

If the goal is to better support children and their families, a family policy agenda is excellent. If the goal is to support the elderly, then a categorical elderly strategy may be more effective. If the goal is to build intergenerational collaboration, then select categorical issues that will be mutually supported across the generations. If the goal is to support diverse cultures, then categorical strategies may be more effective. If the goal is to address poverty, a family policy agenda is an effective strategy. If the goal is to support women, than a family policy agenda can be effective for most women; however, it is not the only strategy that should be used.

Finally, it could be said that the "work" of those that wish to address family policy is to address the basic assumptions or beliefs about families; to define the goals and outcomes that are desired in society; and to develop political strategies to achieve the goals. Perhaps when a nation or state can answer these questions and identify strategies for families, a renaissance will occur - the birth of policies that support individual and families within communities, within states, and within nations. . . the birth of a universal agenda for families.

References

Casey, J. (1989). The History of the Family. New York: Basil Blackwell, Inc.

Dizard J.E. & Gadlin, H. (1990). The Minimal Family. Amherst: The University of Massachusetts Press.

Forsythe, D.P. (1983). Human Rights and World Politics. Lincoln: University of Nebraska Press.

Nelson, B.J. (1985, April). Family politics and policy in the United States and Western Europe. Comparative Politics, pp. 351-371.

Lopez, G.A. & Stohl, M.S. (1989). International Relations: Contemporary Theory and Practice. Washington DC: Congressional Quarterly Press.

Sementilli-Dann, L., Solomon, D., & Tso, K. (1993, January). Investing in Families: The Foundation for the New Economy. Center for Policy Alternatives, Washington, DC.

1994 International Year of the Family, United Nations Office at Vienna, Centre for Social Development and Humanitarian Affairs, Vienna, 1991.

The Proceedings of the Family Supports Roundtable. Center for Policy Alternatives, Washington, DC, December, 1991.

Family Policy: A Global Perspective

Sheila B. Kamerman

Sheila B. Kamerman
Professor
Columbia University School of
Social Work - New York

"When making decisions about providing or cutting back services, governments should consider how these decisions will affect families, directly or indirectly. When services are reduced, apparent savings of public expenditure may conceal great costs in terms of private deprivation, as families struggle to satisfy their needs; likewise, investments in services may be squandered if they fail to take into account the considerations that influence families' ability and willingness to partake of them."

1994 International Year of the Family, "Building the smallest democracy at the heart of society", pg 23. United Nations, Vienna, 1991.

Most national and international statistics define a family in similar terms: *Two or more people related by blood, marriage, or adoption and living together.* In the industrialized countries, the family as it is thought of today is a nuclear family and this pattern is beginning to emerge in developing countries as well (United Nations, 1991). This does not preclude the importance of kinship networks in many subgroups within the industrialized countries and in most developing countries. These networks have been important historically, and still are.

Some historians have suggested that much of the uproar in recent years about the "death" of the family has occurred not out of fear of what will happen to families, but out of society's failure or lack of readiness to adapt to changes. Many of the trends that have been discerned regarding the contemporary family are merely part of an ongoing process, for example, the continued decline in fertility and birth rates. Other trends are occurring globally, not just in the industrialized world. Thus, in both the developed and developing world, women now spend less time married and fewer years bearing and rearing children (United Nations, 1991). Except in a few Asian and African countries, households are getting smaller and have fewer children. Characteristic of the industrialized countries but beginning to emerge in the developing countries as well is "a decline in the strength of kinship and in the importance of family responsibility combined with greater reliance on alternative support systems and greater variations in living arrangements" (United Nations, 1991, p. 4). Most dramatic are the changes in the structure and composition of families and the changes in gender roles, in particular the growth in single-parent, mother-only families headed by divorced or never married women rather than widows, and the rapid rise in paid employment outside of the home for married women with young children (Cherlin, 1988; Duskin, 1990; United Nations, 1991). Yet in child rearing and child socialization, in caregiving and nurturing of elderly and handicapped family members, and - most importantly - in reproducing the future citizenry, the family is, and is likely to continue to be, the primary unit.

State of Present Knowledge

FAMILY POLICY: CONCEPT AND THEORETICAL PERSPECTIVES

The premise undergirding family policy is that society needs children, and needs them to be healthy, well-educated, and, eventually, productive workers, citizens, and parents. There is no generally accepted substitute for the family in its child production and socialization role and there is increasing evidence that nurture and care in a context of love and individualization are essential to achieving the results that society values. The term "family policy" is used to describe what government does to and for children and their families, in particular those public policies (laws, administrative policies) that are designed to affect the situation of families with children - or individuals in their family roles - and those that have clear consequences for such families even though the impacts may not have been intended. In general, the elderly are not included as a part of family policy. Similarly, policies which address youth in their transition to independent adulthood, especially in their entry into the labor force, are not viewed as part of family policy. On the other hand, youth who are still dependent, and youth who are at the stage of forming their own families, are often considered to be a concern of family policies (Kamerman, forthcoming).

The major focus, then, of family policy is children or families with children, especially young children. Characteristic of family policy in the advanced industrialized world is: (1) concern for all children and their families, not just poor families or families with problems, although these and other family types may receive special attention; and (2) an acknowledgment that doing better by children requires help for parents and the family unit as well. In contrast, characteristic of family policies in the developing world is: (1) concern for selected groups of children with serious problems, often street children, handicapped children, migrant children, orphans; and (2) an acknowledgment that public policy must intervene because there are no parents present, or because their capacities are severely constrained. Characteristic of family policies globally is acknowledgment of significant gender role changes, especially changes in women's roles and concern for the consequences of these changes on children and their well-being.

Family policy, therefore, may be explicit or implicit. Explicit family policies include those policies and programs deliberately designed to achieve specific objectives with or for individuals in their family roles or the family unit as a whole. (This does not necessarily mean general agreement as to the objective, but only that the actions are directed toward the family; various actors may have different goals in mind.) Explicit family policies may include population policies (pro- or anti-natalist), income security policies designed to assure families with children a particular standard of living, employment-related benefits for working parents, maternal and child health policies, child care policies, gender equity policies, and so forth. Implicit family policy includes actions taken in other policy domains, for non-family related reasons, but which have important consequences for children and their families as well. For example, an income tax measure designed to raise more revenue may create a work disincentive for a low-earner wife in a husband/wife family; immigration or labor market policies may lead to family separation as men - or women - leave home in search of employment and improved economic opportunities.

Family policy is a subcategory of social policy, and as such can be viewed as a policy field or domain, a policy instrument, or as a perspective or criterion by which all social policies can be assessed as to their consequences for family and child well-being (Kamerman & Kahn, 1978). The family policy field includes those laws that are clearly directed at families, such as: family law; income transfer policies (child or family allowances; AFDC; maternity and parenting benefits); tax benefits for dependents; child care services. Family policy as an instrument may include the same or similar policies, but they are designed to achieve other societal goals. For example, family policy may be used to achieve labor market objectives, encouraging more women to enter the workforce, or discouraging them from entry. Family policies may be designed to encourage parents to bear more children and thus achieve population goals. Family policy may be used to encourage immigration, by assigning family members a priority for entry into a country. Thus, in family policy, the family may be both object and vehicle of social policy.

Family policy as "perspective" assumes that sensitivity to effects and consequences for families inform the public debate about all social policies. Family policy as perspective is concerned with monitoring a broad range of actions in terms of their potential or actual impact on children and their families. Viewing family policies from this vantage point is particularly important in those countries such as the United States, that do not have explicit family policies but rather a series of categorical policy initiatives designed to achieve different and sometimes contradictory objectives and directed toward different aspects of child and family functioning.

On the basis of experience to date, explicit family policies may seek objectives such as the following:
       • to strengthen and support the family economically and otherwise in its child

rearing responsibilities;
- to encourage childbirth and larger families, or to encourage contraceptive use and planned families;
- to facilitate labor force entry of women and mothers and continuity of their labor force attachment, or to facilitate an at-home role for mothers and discourage labor force participation while children are young;
- to protect children;
- to support women's equality;
- to support marriage, or to support child rearing regardless of marital status;
- to facilitate the balancing of work and family life;
- to help the family cope with crises, problems, milestones, and transitions.

Family policy instruments include both cash benefits and services. The major instruments are: income transfers, both cash and tax benefits; maternal and child health policies and programs; parenting policies; child support or maintenance policies; child care policies, both services and various forms of cash and tax subsidies; family law including the laws of inheritance, adoption, guardianship, foster care, marriage, separation, divorce, custody (Glendon, 1977 & 1989); family planning and abortion laws and policy, and related educational and service programs; personal social service programs, both community-based services and residential care for troubled - vulnerable - handicapped children and their families; housing allowances and policies; laws, policies, and programs affecting the status of women; employer and governmental policies affecting work schedules and the interrelationship of work and family life in general.

The domain of implicit family policy (actions which while not specifying a family objective nonetheless have significant family impacts) takes us well beyond these subjects, covering almost anything that government or the private sector might do. This is the case for family policy as "perspective", not in opposition to the more usual policy "field" that includes the various domains mentioned above, but as an addition to it.

Exemplary Action on Behalf of Families

INTERNATIONAL
Illustrations of some of the most important family policies internationally include the following:

• **Income transfer policies** (social insurance, social or public assistance, tax policies, and so forth) can be especially effective in improving the economic well-being of children and their families or reducing or eliminating child poverty (Kamerman & Kahn, 1988). Thus, for example, child poverty rates in the Scandinavian countries, France, Germany, and to a lesser extent Britain and Canada are significantly lower than those in the United States as a result of universal and income-tested child and family allowances, housing allowances, and more generous and uniform public assistance and unemployment benefits. Sixty-three countries, including all the industrialized countries except Turkey, Venezuela and the United States, provided child or family allowances in 1991 (U.S. D.H.H.S., 1992). However, these instruments are far less likely to be used in developing countries primarily because resources are scarcer.

• **Parenting policies** including paid and job-protected leaves from employment for working parents following childbirth or adoption, and sometimes during times of children's illnesses or school transitions, can be especially effective in reducing the tension between family life and work life and in enhancing child development (Kamerman & Kahn, 1991). For example, about 100 countries around the world, including many developing countries, have a paid and job-protected maternity or parenting leave following childbirth. Six to twelve weeks is characteristic of the developing countries. The modal pattern in continental Europe and Canada is about 6 months of paid and job-protected parental leave after birth, while the U.S. has only recently enacted an unpaid parental leave, Australia still has no such policy, and the British policy, although far better than the U.S. policy, is still quite modest and circumscribed. Most view the policy developed in Sweden as the exemplary parenting benefit. The Swedish parent insurance benefit provides for an 18-month job-protected leave following childbirth or adoption, paid at 90 percent of wages for one year and at a modest flat rate for an additional three months. It can be used on a part-time basis by either parent as well. The policy provides for a paid and job-protected leave to care for an ill child and to visit a child's school also, and it continues to have strong support even after the recent election of a conservative government.

   • **Child support or maintenance policies** can be very effective in protecting the economic situation of children in single-parent families. About a dozen European countries including all the Nordic countries, France, Germany, Austria, and Hungary, now provide a guaranteed minimum child support benefit to children in such families, when the non-custodial parent fails to pay support or pays it irregularly or at an inadequate level (Kahn & Kamerman, 1987).

   • **Child care policies and programs** are important for child development purposes, school readiness purposes, as well as to assure child care while parents are employed outside the home. High enrollment rates in good quality preschool programs can be found in France, Italy, and the Nordic countries.

Looking Ahead

ISSUES AND DILEMMAS

   Family policy seems to have arrived internationally as a rubric for organizing alternative views of social policies affecting children and their families. There are public debates in the industrialized countries about alternative family policy agendas; values are discussed and conflicts inevitably surface. The debate still focuses more on what is wrong with families than on how to do better by children, but concern for children is present.

   Nonetheless, there are obstacles and hazards. Among these are:
   • the economic costs, how much the costs are, how and by whom they should be paid;
   • value differences with preferences and choices varying across class, race, ethnic group, religion, gender, age, and so forth;
   • differences regarding the role of government, a particularly important issue for the United States;
   • fear that the development of family policies and programs may serve to undermine the family; and,
   • concern in the advanced industrialized countries that family policy is difficult to develop because the knowledge base is limited and we are not always able to foretell all the consequences.

   It has been suggested elsewhere that it may be more appropriate, some of the time, and closer to the state of knowledge, to specify "bads" or "diswelfare" to be avoided, than to describe specific things to be done and the certainty of achieving desired results.

   Thus the problem. Family policy is difficult: it exposes value conflicts; it reveals disparate philosophies of government; it identifies the varied interests of subgroups in our society; and it reminds us how little we really know. At the same time, family policy is important; and it is inevitable.

Complex modern societies involve a pattern of interdependence which cannot be unraveled. We cannot recreate the earlier family, which was an independent productive unit as well as a consumption unit and which together with its immediate neighborhood managed reasonably well with only temporary outside contact. Our production, technology, patterns of consumption and communication systems have shaped a society dependent upon taxation, road building, housing policy, food inspection, social security systems, police systems, and formal education. Nor can our organized communities, states, and national governments ignore the abused, neglected, parentless, new immigrant, poor children, or the needs of children in families where both parents work, or where there is only one parent.

Inaction, too, is policy. Ultimately, no effective modern society can ignore all response to labor force or family structural change, to demographic trends, or to expanding child poverty. Family policy issues demand agenda space.

Since the problems and needs of families, all kinds of families, continue, the questions and the proposals will persist. The shape of future family policies will reflect what happens to families in different societies, the capacities and resources of the countries concerned, and the values and political choices made in each country. As New York's Senator Moynihan has written and stated repeatedly, the issue is not whether to have family policies but the kind of policies to have.

References

Cherlin, A. (Ed.). (1988). The changing family and family policies. Washington, DC: Urban Institute Press.

Duskin, E. (Ed.). (1990). Lone-parent families: The economic challenge. Paris, France: OECD.

Glendon, M.A. (1977). State, law and family. Amsterdam: North Holland.

Glendon, M.A. (1989). The transformation of family law. Chicago: University of Chicago Press.

Kahn, R., & Kamerman, S. (1987). Child support: From debt collection to social policy. Newbury Park, CA: Sage Publishers.

Kamerman, S.B. (1991). Child care policies and programs: An international overview. In S. Hofferth, & D. Phillips, (Eds.). Child care: A policy and research perspective, Special Issue. Journal of Social Issues, 47(2) 179-196.

Kamerman, S.B. (Forthcoming). Families: Theories and policies, Encyclopedia of Social Work, 19th ed.

Kamerman, S., & Kahn, R. (Eds.). (1978). Family policy: government and families in fourteen countries. New York: Columbia University Press.

Kamerman, S., & Kahn, R. (1988). Social policy and children in the U.S. and Europe. In J. Palmer, T. Smeeding, & B. Torrey (Ed.). The Vulnerable. Washington, DC: Urban Institute Press.

Kamerman, S., & Kahn, R. (Eds.). (1991). Child care, parental leaves, and the under 3s: Policy innovation in Europe. Westport, CT: Auburn House.

Smeeding, T. & Torrey, B.B. (1988). Poor children in rich countries. Science. United Nations, (1991). World's women: Trends and statistics 1970-1990. New York, U.N.

U.S. Department of Health and Human Services. (1992). Social security programs throughout the World - 1991. Washington, DC: Social Security Administration.

Life Course Issues and Family Resources: Preparing for an Uncertain Future

Phyllis Moen & Francille M. Firebaugh

Phyllis Moen
Ferris Family Professor of Life
Course Studies
Cornell University
New York

Francille M. Firebaugh
Dean
College of Human Ecology
Cornell University
New York

A central challenge to families around the world is the disparity between family needs (or claims) and family resources, and how both change over time. Families typically experience difficulty and lack control over their situations when their needs exceed resources; moreover, they undergo need and resource shifts over the life course (Elder, 1981; Moen & Wethington, 1992). Families function effectively when resources enable them to meet their needs and achieve their goals.

Families have a **hierarchy of needs**, with economic and physical security being minimal elements for family effectiveness. Their absence leads to constant apprehension about the uncertain future. But other resources, such as time, are important as well. Envision **trajectories of resources and needs**, and the divergence between the two as families undergo various expected and unexpected transitions. Families move in and out of positions enabling them to mobilize resources and meet needs in the face of external and internal threats. Their spheres of control, and corresponding repertoire of strategies, shift over the life course. Shifts in household composition, family needs, and family resources, along with concomitant shifts in external supports, demands, constraints, and opportunities influence this **control cycle** (Elder & Caspi, 1990). A life course perspective provides a focus on change over the family cycle and across historical time and offers fruitful insights on families, needs and resources.

State of Present Knowledge

First, a life course perspective recognizes the **dynamic nature of family roles and circumstances** as families and individuals move through their lives. This viewpoint uses a "**family career**" concept (Aldous, 1978) where changes in roles, relationships, and responsibilities over time relate to changes in family needs, resources, and vulnerabilities. Families characteristically encounter life course changes in income, economic security, and available time, as well as in their economic and temporal needs. Over the life course, families in advanced countries generally suffer from scarcity in both time and money in the early, childrearing years, become better off financially as they move into middle age, and have more discretionary time in post-retirement years.

In the case of developing countries, many families are goods-poor and time-rich at all life stages, although the gap between needs and material resources creates an absolute scarcity of resources. This scarcity is a constant state of existence for more than one billion people in "acute" poverty (Louat, Grosh & van der Gaag, 1992). In that state, sheer economic deprivation may obscure other strains, such as role conflict and overload. In more advanced economies, the intersection of roles, such as those of worker and parent, may well generate strains and challenges for families related to time as well as money.

Second, life experiences and life choices among family members are **interdependent**. Family members choices, or the circumstances thrust upon them, have repercussions that reverberate throughout the family system, including across generations (Bronfenbrenner, 1990). Interdependence in terms of the family economy means that the household is an income-pooling unit, sharing in some ways both prosperity and adversity (Moen, Kain & Elder, 1983). In developing countries, however, the notion of shared prosperity and adversity may be more assumed than real.

Assistance programs that differentially benefit individuals rather than whole families can shift the household's sharing, thereby altering a program's effect on the

*"Together, familial produc-
tivity in the household and
on the job and familial
consumption keep a na-
tional economy active. The
national economy, in turn,
provides the income and
support systems that maintain families and sustain
their welfare."*

United Nations Occasional Papers
Series, No. 5, 1993. "Family as an
Enviroment: an Ecosystem Perspec-
tive on Family Life", pg 6.

family as a whole (Louat, Grosh & van der Gaag, 1992). Moreover, gender-related social and cultural practices may allow men to keep more income for themselves if they discontinue support to wives and children, thus promoting progressive detachment of men from women and children (Garfinkel & McLanahan, 1986). Income controlled by women in many settings is associated with larger expenditures devoted to children's well-being (e.g., nutrition, health, and education) than is income controlled by men (Blumberg, 1993).

Interdependence underscores the affective concern of family members for one another as well as their sense of moral obligation to care for, as well as care about one another. Families are not only childrearing systems but also informal care providers for the aged and the infirm (Litwak, 1985; Mogey, 1990; Stack, 1974). An estimated 80 to 90 percent of health care in the United States comes from family members, especially wives, daughters, and daughters-in-law (U.S. House of Representatives Select Commit-tee on Aging, 1988).

Third, the **historical and cultural contexts** constitute **situational imperatives** to which families must respond. Families and individuals of the 1990s face the effects of macro-political, economic and demographic realities: growing nationalism and ethnocentrism, economic depression, globalization of markets, high structural unem-ployment, increased migration and refugee populations, increased life expectancies and fertility. The impact of these situational imperatives on families will differ considerably from the constraints and opportunities faced by families of the 1930s or 1950s. Both expected life transitions -- parenthood, retirement, a geographical move -- and unex-pected crisis events -- unemployment, floods, war mobilization, illness, death -- can place families in crisis. Cultural and subcultural considerations further shape the available life choices and opportunities.

Fourth, early life experience plays out in the **cumulation of advantage (or disadvantage)** over the life course (Elder & Caspi, 1990). Thus families with initial material, social or cultural resources typically employ their resources to the continuing advantage of all family members. By contrast, families consisting of women and their children typically possess only marginal resources and are particularly vulnerable to a downward spiral. The World Bank documents how women bear more of the effects of poverty, shouldering more of the workload than men, with less education, and less access to remunerative activities.

Children across the world, including the United States, suffer disproportionately, being more likely to be poor than any other subgroup. Changing family structures, desertion and absence of fathers, divorce and single parenthood, magnify economic difficulties. Poor children in many developing countries face poverty compounded by inadequate nutrition, health care, and education. Girls are generally more disadvan-taged than boys, with enrollment in primary schooling less than 50 percent in many African countries (Louat, Grosh & van der Gaag, 1992).

Consider the growing numbers of poor preschoolers in the United States. Throughout the 1970s the proportion of children in poverty stayed at between 17 and 18 percent; it climbed in the 1980s, and by 1991 it was at 24 percent (National Center for Children in Poverty, 1993). Children under six in the United States are more likely than any age group to be poor, while racial and ethnic poverty differences among children are striking: African-American, 51 percent; Hispanic-American, 44 percent; Whites, 14 percent. The poverty rate for young children with single mothers was 59 percent in 1991, compared to 13 percent for two-parent families.

Fifth, families and family members are **active participants** in the larger society, participants who respond to, rework, or reframe external constraints and opportunities. Rather than being compliant, submissive units, families and households are flexible, decision-making units, actively choosing various patterns of behavior.

Exemplary Action on Behalf of Families

In Finland, new parents are provided with a complete layette for their infant. This makes sense economically, in helping families during this important transition, but also makes a statement as to the value of children to the broader community. Such a focus on supporting effective families is characteristic of policies in Scandinavia and in Europe generally. By contrast, government policies in the United States frequently respond to the situational imperatives confronting families in trouble -- in the form of **crisis events**, such as unemployment, hurricanes or floods, and **ongoing strains**, such as low income or a family member with a disability.

Clearly, the best actions are those related to prevention, that stave off crises and strains in the first place. For example, Sweden has historically not let its unemployment rate rise above about 3 percent, and provides subsidized job training to those who do become unemployed. Thus most Swedish families don't experience unemployment in the ways that, say, Brazilian families do. Another example of preventative action is health care, provided through various means in every advanced nation except the United States and South Africa. Yet another example is assuring the financial security of single-parent families. Austria, France, Denmark and Sweden have "advance maintenance payments" for child support when one parent is absent. Each month a tax is levied on all absent parents and that is redistributed in the form of a minimum payment to all children with an absent parent (Rodgers, 1990).

Communities and volunteers are actively involved in staving off strains, as exemplified by a successful in-home support service of visiting and respite care in one region in the United States: Southeastern Pennsylvania. In the intergenerational program, well elders and high school or college students are matched with caregiving families and isolated elders and children with special needs (Henkin, 1991).

Such exemplary policies and programs tend to recognize the ebb and flow of family resources and needs. Two stages of the family cycle are times of heightened vulnerability -- the post-retirement years and the early years of childbearing and childrearing. And two resources are crucial to family effectiveness: money and time.

The United States has a policy to promote the welfare and well-being of its elderly families, as exemplified in Social Security legislation and Medicare. These are policies that worked; elderly Americans are less likely to be poor in the early 1990s than was the case in the 1930s or 1950s. Their sense of uncertainty about the future is very much assuaged by the economic supports of social security and the comfort of assured medical care. What is required is such creative solutions for the new realities of poverty in America: poor children and their families, which, frequently, consist of single parent mothers.

The Earned Income Tax Credit adopted by Congress in 1993 is just such a creative solution; supporting working families whose jobs do not provide a "living wage." The Family Support Act of 1988 was also designed to promote independence rather than dependence, aiming to help prepare welfare recipients for employment and to provide them with supportive services through a period of education and training. A major requirement is that mothers of young children are required to stay in high school, be employed, or undergo job training as a condition for receiving Aid to Families with Dependent Children.

Another exemplary solution is one making both parents financially responsible for their children. In a number of countries, non-custodial parents, most frequently fathers, are increasingly subject to more stringent methods of enforcing child support obligations. Australia, for example, has introduced a two-stage program for reform in child support collection procedures, resulting in increased collections (Harrison, 1991). And the Family Support Act strengthens child-support enforcement procedures in the United States. Single parenthood's effects on both poverty and children are inconsistent from a cross-national perspective. Women-headed households are generally, although not universally, poorer than male-headed ones. In a number of studies, children in women-headed households were better nourished than in the case of male-headed (two parent) families, even when the effects of income were accounted for (Blumberg, 1993). Data from African countries point to the large amount of women's reproductive life course spent without a spouse or partner in residence, with fathers only marginally involved with their children (Bruce & Lloyd, 1992). Policies providing children access to the resources of both parents are clearly crucial for effective childrearing, as are policies to involve fathers in the day-to-day upbringing of their children and to promote the ability of women to obtain adequate earnings (Bruce & Lloyd, 1992).

Yet another form of exemplary action concerns the reconciliation, for both men and women, of the conflicts between work and family role obligations. European countries have developed a number of supports, in the form of paid parental leave, child care, children's allowance, and time off from work to care for sick children. Botswana provides 50 percent of the gross salary for 12 weeks for women workers for maternity leave and there are proposals to extend the paid leave (Carr, 1991).

The parental leave debate in the United States in the 1980s and early 1990s stands in marked contrast to that of other advanced nations. The Family and Medical Leave Act of 1993 provides 12 weeks of unpaid (with health benefits continued), job-protected leave per year for the birth or adoption of a child or for the serious illness of the employee or an immediate family member. However, employers with fewer than 50 employees (accounting for about 60% of the workforce) are exempt.

Scandinavian countries lead in fashioning exemplary policies, such as extended paid parental leave for both parents, that both promote equality between men and women and relieve the strains on working families. Yet even in Sweden it is women who continue to have the primary responsibility for home and family care (Moen, 1989; Haas, 1992). Likewise, women who work in the agricultural systems in developing countries spend a great deal of time in household and agricultural production.

Looking Ahead

We suggest four broad areas of family functioning where public policies can potentially enhance family effectiveness; encouraging family formation and stability, sustaining the family economy, strengthening the family as a socializing unit, and fortifying the family as a caregiving unit. The issue is how to fashion policies that promote family resilience rather than dependency.

A life course approach can inform the development of exemplary family policies in at least three ways. First, social policies expanding or restricting the family's strategies of adaptation can have enduring, and possibly unanticipated, influences. Government programs such as entitlements may foster a cumulative relative advantage or disadvantage over time, according to their timing in the family's life course. In the United States we have seen that means-tested programs (such as Aid to Families with Dependent Children) frequently foster dependency; non-stigmatized entitlements, on the other hand, (such as the Earned Income Tax Credit) advance independence. The goal should be to **prevent** families from getting into difficulty in the first place, rather than attempting to "fix" them once they are already in trouble.

Second, a life course approach can help policy makers place families and policies in suitable historical contexts. Too frequently policies are framed by looking backwards, rather than forward. If we do look forward we see two changes that must be on the family policy agenda in the United States as we move toward the next century: the reality of **dual-earner and single-parent families**, requiring policies making it possible for working mothers and fathers to combine their work and family responsibilities, and the **revolution in longevity**, necessitating policies addressing family caregiving, the retirement years, and long-term health care. Both these social transformations become increasingly critical as the large baby boom cohort moves first into raising families and then into the later years of adulthood.

Third, a life course awareness can help in identifying factors affecting family needs and/or family resources. For example, women-headed families are especially vulnerable to economic privation, and times of transition -- as families move into parenthood, divorce, caregiving, retirement -- frequently are also times of strain. From a policy perspective, the issue is how to maximize the effectiveness of families with different strengths and resources who confront different challenges and to determine under what circumstances advantages or disadvantages accumulate.

Throughout the world, public policies that do take families into account focus mostly on the family economy, and, given our notion of the hierarchy of needs, economic security **is** paramount. But families need other resources as well, such as health care, time, skills, support, and information. Moreover, the intrafamily relationships and allocation practices that affect family members differently cannot be ignored. Families as active and dynamic institutions can, for the most part, be effective in caring for dependents (children, disabled adults, and infirm elderly), in promoting the optimal development of the next generation, and as economically viable units -- at all stages of the life course. But families can operate effectively only to the degree they are equipped with the requisite resources as they move through time. What is required are public policies that help families sustain their private lives and uphold a sense of certainty, rather than uncertainty, about the contours of their future.

References

Aldous, J. (1978). Family Careers. New York: Wiley.

Bronfenbrenner, U. (1990). Discovering what families do. In D. Blankenhorn, S. Bayme, J. B. Elshtan (Eds.) Rebuilding the nest: A new commitment to the American family, (pp. 27-38). Milwaukee, WI: Family Service America.

Blumberg, R.L. (1993). Poverty versus 'Purse Power': The political economy of the mother-child family III. In J. P. Mencher and A. Okongwu (Eds.). Where did all the men go? (pp. 13-52). Boulder, CO: Westview Press.

Bruce, J. & Lloyd, C.B. (1992). Family research and policy issues for the 1990s. In IFPRI Policy Briefs 8. Understanding how resources are allocated within households. Washington, DC: International Food Policy Research Institute, The World Bank.

Carr, M. (1991). Women and food security. London: Intermediate Technology Publications.

Elder, G.H., Jr. & Caspi, A. (1990). Studying lives in a changing society: Sociological and personological explorations. In Rabin, et al (Eds.), Studying persons and lives, (pp.201-247). New York: Springer.

Elder, G. H., Jr. (1981). History and the family: The discovery of complexity. Journal of Marriage and the Family, 43 489-519.

Garfinkel, I., & McLanahan, S. (1986). Single Mothers and Their Children. Washington, DC: Urban Institute Press.

Haas, L. (1992). Equal parenthood and social policy: A study of parental leave in Sweden. Albany, NY: State University of New York Press.

Harrison, M. (1991). The reformed Australian child support scheme. Journal of Family Issues, 12, 430-449.

Henkin, N. Z. (1991). Resourceful aging: Today and tomorrow, Conference Proceedings, 3, 39-44.

Louat, F., Grosh, M., & van der Gaag, J. (1992). Understanding how resources are allocated within households. IFPRI Policy Briefs 8. Washington, DC: International Food Policy Research Institute, The World Bank.

Litwak, E. (1985). Helping the elderly: The contemporary roles of informal networks and formal systems. New York: Guilford Press.

Moen, P. (1989). Working parents: Transformations in gender roles and public policies in Sweden. Madison, WI: University of Wisconsin Press.

Moen, P., Kain, E., & Elder, G.H. (1983). Economic conditions and family life: Contemporary and historical perspectives. In J. Nelson & F. Skidmore (Eds.), American families and the economy: The high costs of living, (pp. 213-259). Washington, DC: National Academy Press.

Moen, P., & Wethington, E. (1992). Family adaptation strategies. Annual review of sociology, 18, 233-51.

Mogey, J. (1990). Aiding and aging: The coming crisis in support for the elderly by kin and state. New York: Greenwood.

National Center for Children in Poverty. (1992). Five million children: 1992 update. Columbia University School of Public Health.

Rodgers, Jr., H. R. (1990). Poor women, poor families. Armonk, NY: M.E. Sharpe, Inc.

Stack, C. B. (1974). All our kin: Strategies for survival in a black community. New York: Harper and Row.

U. S. House of Representatives Select Committee on Aging. (1988). Exploding the myths: Caregiving in America. No. 100-665. Washington, DC: U.S. Government Printing Office.

A Child Is Born:
Conception, Fertility and Childbearing

Greer Litton Fox

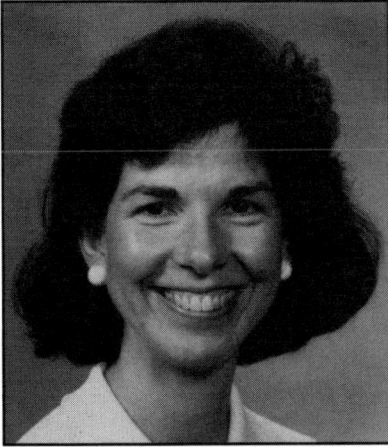

Greer Litton Fox
Distinguished Professor of
Family Studies
University of Tennessee

The birth of a healthy child to willing and able parents is the occasion for community celebration the world over. The historical and anthropological literatures are replete with descriptions of sacred and secular ceremonies that mark the event of birth. Truly, there are few experiences that are as universally associated with joy, anticipation, and shared promise as the birth of a child. And it is equally difficult to name another human experience that falls so short of our hopes as the conception, gestation, and birth of children in the late 20th century.

Several issues surrounding conditions of birth and well-being of infants and young children around the world will be reviewed, using the concept of "optimal conditions for childbearing" as an organizing rubric. Optimal conditions refer neither to ideal maximum conditions for life nor to the least that is needed to sustain life. Instead, "optimal" is the hypothetical point of compromise between necessity and excess. It is important to acknowledge that the identification of optimal conditions depends upon one's perspective: The perspectives of the mother, the child, the father, the birth nation, and the world community may differ. In the remainder of the essay, actual conditions for childbearing will be measured against optimal conditions. A next step is to identify which of the factors hindering optimal childbearing can be addressed effectively by the family, the nation, or the international community. And the programs that foster hope in achieving optimal outcomes for children and lend themselves to successful replication elsewhere can be described.

State of Present Knowledge

THE PERSPECTIVE OF THE MOTHER

Optimally, becoming a mother is a choice made by a woman. Exposure to episodes of sexual intercourse, including those which carry the risk of conception, should be an act of choice on the part of the woman. The sexual assault and sexual violation of women, whether as an intentional policy of war or as unplanned acts of sexual aggression, are generally repudiated as abhorrent within the family, the nation, and the international community. In the United States, almost 13 percent of white and 8 percent of unmarried black teenage girls report having experienced a forced sexual encounter (Moore, Nord, & Peterson, 1989). Our laws reflect the goal to reduce to zero both the numbers of women subjected to rape and the number of conceptions that result from forced sexual contact.

A second optimal condition for childbearing from the mother's perspective is choice in timing, spacing, and numbers of children. Accessibility to effective and affordable methods of family planning along with information about human sexuality are needed to insure this choice for mothers. The United Nations Population Fund estimates that currently more than 500 million women around the globe lack access to quality family planning (World Population News Service, 1992). Given the positive benefits of planned childbearing to families and for children, the enormous gap between desired and available services poses a challenge for the international community in the years ahead. Freedom of choice in conception and contraception also includes the freedom from forced pregnancy termination. Some nations employ population policies that rely upon coerced termination of desired intentional pregnancies. Coercion in conception, childbearing or pregnancy termination is unacceptable.

A third optimal condition from the perspective of mothers is for a healthy and

"Full, informed and joint participation in family planning decisions by both spouses appears to be essential to a responsible choice and a wider sharing of familial roles and responsibilities."

1994 International Year of the Family. "Building the smallest democracy at the heart of society", pg 17. United Nations, Vienna, 1991.

protected pregnancy. Women are uniquely vulnerable during pregnancy, and optimally a community exerts great effort to value and sustain women during this period. The provision of medical care and appropriate nutrition to pregnant women is a vital safeguard for their future health and for the development of their newborn. In some parts of the world, the ability of women to sustain a healthy pregnancy is also compromised by traditional cultural practices of genital mutilation. As a matter of basic human rights as well as of health care for women, cultures with these traditions are experiencing vigorous pressure to discontinue their practice. In other parts of the world, the well being of pregnant women and their unborn children is threatened by the violent behavior of husbands or male partners; unfortunately, this behavior is not so universally discouraged. Finally, we note that maternal mortality, that is, the risk of dying from pregnancy-related causes, is a grave concern in many parts of the globe. Asian women face a 1 in 54 chance of dying and African women a 1 in 21 chance of dying during pregnancy or childbirth (Yinger, 1990). The sources of risk are many and they differ among communities and from nation to nation. The protection of women during pregnancy and childbirth is optimally a community-wide responsibility, which can be discharged through programs that address the risks specific to each community setting.

THE PERSPECTIVE OF THE CHILD

Optimal conditions for childbearing from the perspective of a child include being wanted at conception, being born healthy, and being born to willing and able parents. Not only can the wantedness of children be most nearly assured by giving conceptive and contraceptive choice to their mothers and fathers, but wantedness also increases when a culture shifts from property or instrumental interests in children to person-centered interests. Children deserve to be valued for their own individual uniqueness. Instead, in many settings around the world, they are valued because they contribute to the material wealth and well-being of their lineage or kin group, or because they are born of one gender and not the other, or because of their anticipated potential contributions to family or household well-being via their labor or marriage. Valuing the uniqueness of each human life need not be in opposition to the familistic values of the lineage or kin group.

The first year of life is a critical indicator of the true valuation of children by a community. The proportion of children ever born who survive to their first birthday varies tremendously within and across nations (Population Reference Bureau, 1991). Given limited economic and medical resources, it seems more appropriate to target programs to increase the proportion of children who reach age one than to focus on the survivability of fetuses with ever shorter gestational ages. Programs such as the USDA WIC program and others which invest in the nutritional needs of infants and children should be supported, encouraged, and extended.

Lucky is the child born to willing parents, but for optimal outcomes for children, the parents must also be able to parent. One of the factors most critical in child health and well-being is the educational level of the mother (WPNS, 1993). Education programs especially targeted to young women, such as those in CARE and the Christian Children's Fund, have remarkable payoffs in positive outcomes for children. The vulnerability of children is closely attached to the vulnerability of women, so policies that enhance women's economic strengths both within and outside the home rebound positively for children. Cross-national research on household economics shows that children fare better nutritionally in households in which income is controlled by mothers rather than fathers (Blumberg, 1991). The extension of parenting education and household management training to parents of both genders may foster heightened sensitivity to the needs of the most vulnerable members of their families and households.

A traditional Ashanti proverb holds that "it takes a village to raise a child." This ancient wisdom directs our attention to the community responsibility for providing backup systems of care for their children. Thus, informal adoption, safe houses for victimized children, temporary foster care, orphanages for children temporarily or permanently separated from parents, and formal adoption are all alternative forms of parenting care for children. When substitutes for birth parents are needed, children must have ready access to alternative settings within their communities for growth and development.

THE PERSPECTIVE OF THE FATHER

Evolutionary psychologists assert that men are predisposed to perpetuation of their own unique genetic makeup through reproduction (Daly & Wilson, 1988). Optimal conditions for childbearing from the perspective of the father, according to this model, would include certainty of paternity through absolute control over his wife's (wives') sexual exposure, and exclusive preoccupation of his wife with the bearing and rearing of his and only his children. These conditions insure that his efforts to sustain the viability of his family would be exclusively invested in his and only his genetic potential. The extension of literacy, economic opportunity, and reproductive independence to women threaten men's interests, according to this model, and resistance to such social changes - which can be seen throughout the world - is predictable.

In a human development model, the optimal conditions for childbearing from the father's perspective highlight his ability to parent effectively rather than simply procreate efficiently. Thus, a community which provides support and recognition of men's contributions to the health and well-being of children, an economic structure which not only provides jobs, but job flexibility sufficient to allow for fathers' involvement in day-to-day care and activities with children, an educational infrastructure which emphasizes skill building in human relationships as well as technical and literacy skills for both genders, and economic activities that provide rewards sufficient to sustain one's family all are optimal conditions for healthy child outcomes from a father's perspective. It is notable that in the family planning efforts of several countries (e.g., Turkey, Kenya), the involvement of men in family planning decision-making has been found to be essential to the successful implementation and widespread adoption of effective contraceptive and family planning measures (World Population News Service, 1993). The articulation of the responsibilities, rights, and rewards of increased parental involvement in the lives of their infants and children can enhance the father role for men around the world.

THE PERSPECTIVE OF THE BIRTH NATION

Throughout history, kings, warlords and leaders -- malevolent or benevolent -- have defined national power in terms of population size. From the vantage point of the birth nation, optimal conditions for childbearing have traditionally been defined in terms of the maximization of birth rates; and in many parts of the globe, this perspective still dominates. Increasingly however, many nations have come to recognize a balance or trade-off between quantity and quality of the national population. Investments in children's health, education, and care in their early years reap long-term profits through a productive and healthy citizenry. Unfortunately, even today nation-states are rift by ethnic conflict, and the bodies of children are all too often the chosen battlegrounds for these conflicts. As a matter of deliberate public policy, food, shelter, medical care, and security are being systematically withheld from certain groups of children (e.g., Bosnia, Sudan, Somalia). In other nations, the disparities of fate and fortune have created a similar outcome, such that the life chances of children differ radically by race, religion, and ethnicity (e.g., the USA, Japan, United Kingdom).

Whether a given nation can sustain itself as an integrated whole when portions of its citizenry live well at the expense of others is a question that looms in the future of many nations, both large and small, developed or developing, democratic and totalitarian.

Looking Ahead

THE PERSPECTIVE OF THE WORLD COMMUNITY

In some respects the most serious issue facing the world community is the lack of balance between population growth and natural and human-produced resources. There are grave disparities among nations in the life chances of their children, in the distribution of resources for supporting their children, and in the rates of population growth in those regions. The developed countries account for just over one-fifth of the human population and are growing very slowly; yet this small segment of the Earth's people controls the majority of the globe's resources. Ironically, the populations of most impoverished nations are growing rapidly and their very young populations are increasingly devastated by shortages of food and other resources necessary for sustaining life. In these countries, children are a precious and valued resource sustaining the hopes and constituting the wealth of their families and communities.

Thus, we have a situation in which the children of one portion of the globe threaten seriously the survival of all because of their <u>numbers</u>. Although the needs of each child are met with a meager share of the world's resources, their sheer numbers will soon outweigh our ability to sustain them. The other portion of the world's children threaten us because of the <u>excess</u>. Although few in number, their exorbitant claims on the world's resources also pose a threat to the survival of all. Aside from the justification of raw power -- demographic, economic, political, or military -- one is hard pressed to justify the claims of one group over the other.

The long-term survival of the human population on this planet may well depend on addressing the threat to survival posed by each group of children. That is, on the one hand we must address the extremely high rates of population growth in some areas. In so doing, there is reason to be hopeful: Four of the most effective strategies for reducing population growth also foster optimal outcomes for children. These strategies include programs that:

1. Reduce infant and child mortality.
2. Increase educational opportunities, targeting young girls and women specifically in literacy programs.
3. Provide access to safe, affordable, and effective family planning services.
4. Improve family income through sustained economic development opportunities.

Recognition of the complex interplay among the factors involved in spiraling population growth can pinpoint several vital points for intervention (World Population News Service, 1993).

There is also an equally important second arena for action. The materialistic ideology that drives the developed nations must be addressed as a threat to human survival. Alternative bases for self worth and social status must be defined to replace those that value the accumulation of material wealth and consumer goods. The religious, philosophical, and ethical systems in cultures of scarcity are the likely source of such alternative conceptualizations of the value of human life. Sensitive contact across cultural, ethnic, racial, and national lines can encourage the discovery and sharing of alternative views of life meaning and well-being. However, economic hegemony is usually accompanied by a high degree of cultural arrogance, and outcomes of intercultural exchange are often asymmetrical: The cultures of scarcity have been more likely to adopt the value systems and aspire to the ways of life of the cultures of abundance than vice versa. International leadership on this issue is needed.

The problematic combination of unbridled population growth and economic hegemony and domination of world resources have together created a savage disparity in life chances for children around the world. Unless both sides of this conundrum are addressed simultaneously, the continued provision of optimal conditions for childbearing and healthy child outcomes cannot be guaranteed for any of the world's children.

References

Blumberg, R.L. (1991). Gender family and economy - The triple overlap. Newbury Park: Sage.

Daly, M., & Wilson, M. (1988). Homicide. New York: Aldine de Gruyter.

Moore, K.A., Nord, C.W., & Peterson, J.L. (1989). Nonvoluntary sexual activity among adolescents. Family Planning Perspectives, 21(3), 110-114.

Population Reference Bureau. (1991). World population data sheet 1990. Washington, DC.

World Population News Service. (1992, November-December). Dr. Sadik urges local community involvement. Popline, 14, 1-2.

World Population News Service. (1993, January-February). Male responsibility. Popline, 15, 4.

World Population News Service (1993, January-February). Reducing growth protects children. Popline, 15, 1-2.

Yinger, N. (1990). Focus on maternal mortality. Population Today, 18(5), 6-9.

Healthy Families in Healthy Cities: A Global Responsibility

Beverly Collora Flynn & Louise Ivanov Dennis

Beverly Collora Flynn, Ph.D.,
R.N., FAAN
Professor, School of Nursing
Indiana University

Viewing families as the basic elements of society suggests one appropriate way to create supportive environments using the community perspective. The Healthy Cities movement, which began in the European Region of the World Health organization (WHO) in 1986, emphasizes this approach. The city is viewed as the level of government closest to the people and establishes a process in which community leaders from different sectors of life work together to improve their community's health. Healthy Cities incorporates a broad definition of health, one that emphasizes prevention of community problems and the development of individuals and families. Health encompasses all aspects of life including housing, education, religion, employment, nutrition, leisure and recreation, health and medical care, and a clean environment. Healthy cities emphasizes the reduction of inequalities in health status and in access to the prerequisites for health; the development of healthy public policies at the local level; the creation of physical and social environments that support health; the strengthening of community action for health; and, a reorientation of health services in accordance with the goal of "health for all by the year 2000" and the principles of health promotion (Flynn et al., 1991; Tsouros, 1990; WHO, 1978; WHO, 1986). These concepts are consistent with those found in the family literature which include the ecological approach to family health, building on family strengths, interdisciplinary collaboration, and community participation (Chamberlin, 1992).

State of Present Knowledge

Louise Ivanov Dennis, MSN, RN
Associate Professor, School of
Nursing
Indiana University

Cities, which in many respects are worlds apart, share a common bond by being Healthy Cities and addressing common concerns, that of issues related to family health. The cities of Vienna, Austria; Glasgow, Scotland; Gothenburg, Sweden; St. Petersburg, Russia; and Clark County, Indiana (formerly the Jeffersonville Healthy City) are committed to addressing family issues through Healthy Cities. Describing the experiences of these cities exemplifies what we know about these issues, how different settings respond within their cultural and economic limits, and allows us to see what is yet to be achieved. In this essay, we consider what is known about adolescent sexuality, women and the elderly and then describe exemplary programs for these three categories. The health of individuals and the health of families is interdependent with the community as will be illustrated.

ADOLESCENTS AND SEXUALITY: HEALTH RELATED CONCERNS

Adolescence is a period in life that can be defined as an era with biopsychosocial dimensions that begins with a focus on the individual and shifts to able participation in the family, society, and culture. This shift can be enhanced by creating supportive environments within society. Frequently however, there is a discrepancy in societal expectations of adolescents and biopsychological development; for example, in relation to the development of sexuality. In industrialized societies, development of sexuality is assumed to occur during adolescence with the development of sex characteristics which leads to the expectation that they will become responsible sexual actors. The interesting contradiction that is apparent within industrial societies is that adolescents are defined as sexually mature, while at the same time socially and psychologically immature (Adelson & Doehrman, 1980). Creating supportive environments within societies can help bridge the schism between sexual maturity and social and psychological maturity, thereby preparing adolescents to become responsible members of society.

St. Petersburg, Russia and Clark County, Indiana have a common concern, that of teenage pregnancy, and are addressing adolescent pregnancy issues through Healthy Cities. St. Petersburg, with a population of 5 million people is involved in profound political, economic, and social change. In 1991, the maternal mortality rate was an alarming 69.4 per 100,000 live births (Wagoner, 1992). Of these, 7.2% were women 20 years of age and younger (Kirichenko, 1992). Reasons given for the high mortality rate are that maternity care is highly medicalized and contraception is unavailable resulting in high abortion rates (Tusheva, 1992; Draper et al. 1992). The rate of abortion is 1 live birth to 2 abortions with abortions among women 17 years of age and younger steadily increasing (Tusheva, 1992). In the absence of contraception teens resort to abortion as a means of contraception resulting in a high incidence of gynecologically related problems (Gurkin, 1992).

In Clark County 16.2% of all births in 1989 were to teenage mothers 19 years or younger, with 87.5% to white teens and 12.5% to nonwhite. Because areas with small populations frequently result in unstable rates, the moving rates over several years were calculated for teen mothers. The moving fertility rate for teens was 31.2 per 1,000 female teenagers in 1987-1989. The teenage pregnancy rates continue to rise with a moving rate of 56.1 per 1,000 teen females for 1987-1990. The maternal mortality rate for the County was zero in 1987-1989. The moving abortion rates for Clark County were 9.45 per 1,000 teen births in 1985-1989 (Indiana State Department of Health, 1990)! These data are not considered accurate because teenagers also have abortions across the Ohio River in Kentucky where there is no parental consent law (which Indiana has). In addition, the abortions in Kentucky are not recorded in Indiana. Abortion rates available for the United States (28 per 1,000 women in 1985) and the former Soviet Union (181 per 1,000 women in 1982) indicate different public orientations toward abortion in the two societies (Abortion Report, 1992).

WOMEN: HEALTH RELATED CONCERNS

Women's health and policy issues have become more visible as women worldwide struggle for equal visibility in health-related and policy concerns specific to women. Fueling this visibility in the united States is the growing number of women entering the workforce and heading single households, thereby creating unique health issues and problems that have received little attention. Much of the research conducted has used men as subjects assuming that women's biopsychosocial development is similar to men's. In addition to specific problems of women such as a rising incidence of breast cancer and hysterectomies, women's health problems are beginning to mirror those of men in areas related to stress, heart disease, and lung cancer. An interdisciplinary approach to women's health can help to provide the supportive environment necessary to deal with health and policy issues specific to women.

THE ELDERLY: HEALTH RELATED CONCERNS

As the life span increases in much of the Western world, health related concerns unique to an aging population develop. One such concern is what to do with aging parents. Unlike that of developing countries, families living in the West are more mobile and less likely to have aging parents living with them. Currently in the United States, the elderly comprise 12 percent of the population with 1 percent of the population 85 and older (U.S. Senate Special Committee on Aging, 1991).

Aging requires community programs that can address the needs of both the active and frail elderly. Inappropriate housing and lack of integrated community care are serious barriers to creating a supportive environment for independence and quality of life for the elderly in cities.

"Increased attention may be called for in promoting the role of families in meeting the health requirements of all their members and in primary health care, child and maternal health and food security."

1994 International Year of the Family. "Building the smallest democracy at the heart of society", pg 16. United Nations, Vienna, 1991.

Exemplary Action on Behalf of Families

THE HEALTHY CITIES MOVEMENT: ADOLESCENTS

In both St. Petersburg and Clark County local leaders involved in Healthy Cities identified adolescent pregnancy as a priority issue. They saw their responsibility as creating an environment that promotes healthy adolescents for responsible roles in society. Although the approaches differ, the solutions developed are unique to each setting.

In St. Petersburg, a Center for Reproductive Health Services for Teenagers was started in 1991. The focus of the Center is medical care, sex education, and social activities. The Center provides free medical services to adolescent girls including gynecologic, endocrine, cardiac, psychologic, cosmetology and plastic surgery. Abortions also are performed, and all girls seeking an abortion receive counseling with a psychologist before and after the abortion. Sex education and contraceptive use is taught by gynecologists to all girls who come to the Center. A telephone crisis line is answered by a psychologist 12 hours each day. Currently adolescent girls use the Center as a place to gather where they can discuss sexual, social, and psychological issues among themselves and with professionals. Future plans for the Center include adding medical services for adolescent boys and including them in the sex education classes. Free contraceptives and literature on contraception, sexually transmitted diseases, and AIDS also are in the projected plans for the Center, as are support groups for girls choosing abortion. Many of the Center's activities may change if the plans for the St. Petersburg school curricula change to include sex education, psychosexuality, reproduction and contraception. Eventually the Center will add a sports complex where adolescents can gather under the supervision of adults for fun, exercise, and emotional support.

The members of the Healthy City Committee in Clark County expressed concern that teenage parents should be encouraged to remain in school since education is so crucial to the future of the teen and the child. They found that up to 20 students drop out of school in one year to care for their children in the local high school of 2,000 students. In any given year it is estimated there are about 40 student parents at the school (Teen and Tots at School, 1992). The school nurse spearheaded the effort and worked with the local high school to develop a Teen and Tots Program. The program offers childcare services for student parents in a center at the school and provides a supportive environment for teens to complete their education. Also included is a course for vocational students to learn about child care and parenting. Time is spent in classrooms learning about basic needs and health of young children, and in getting hands-on experiences by working in the day care facility. Teens also learn how much work is needed to take care of a child, in addition to the effect it has on one's lifestyle. The in-school day care involves both teenage parents in the parenting and healthy baby classes.

THE HEALTHY CITIES MOVEMENT: WOMEN

Vienna is at the cutting edge of the health promoting hospitals movement. The Vienna Healthy City project organized the Women's Health Centre which has political support and contracts with a hospital, the organizing research institute, the city of Vienna, and the World Health Organization. The Centre aims to reorient health services towards health promotion and local needs by providing a range of health services specific to women. Research is used to identify the needs of women and to establish appropriate services. At the same time the Centre prepares various female professionals for women's health services. In addition, three female psychologists working in a team offer counseling to young girls in schools, women who are dependent on tranquilizers, and offer support to middle-aged women. The Centre is open to members of the community and sponsors seminars, lectures, and courses (Draper et al., 1992).

THE HEALTHY CITIES MOVEMENT: ELDERLY

Gothenburg, Sweden, Healthy City has developed a comprehensive strategy for the care of older people based on extensive research into the elderly's living conditions. Not surprising was the fact that most of the elderly wanted to remain in their homes. A policy was established that promoted 2,000 new housing places for the elderly in the 1990s. The aims of the policy included enabling people to remain in their homes; developing group housing and homes that provided 24 hour medical care; encouraging skilled primary care; providing access to qualified home help; providing care at geriatric psychogeriatric clinics. The policy provided avenues to redistribute and provide new resources to meet the needs of people over the age of 80. In Sweden, responsibility for the implementation of the policy depends on the effective development of activities at the local level as well as collaboration among city departments. Local pensioners' consultation groups also are involved in the implementation of the policy. Self help groups are involved in the development of community facilities for the elderly such as visiting services, walking groups, and study circles (Draper et al., 1992).

Looking Ahead

Cities throughout the world are faced with current pressing problems resulting from inadequate primary prevention, and inadequate housing and community services. Cultural values in societies can prevent an open and rational dialogue for creative problem solving, resulting in a situation of downstream thinking. (Downstream thinking addresses the consequences rather than the causes or precursors of the problem, which is upstream thinking.) In upstream thinking, issues are addressed on how to create supportive environments to help people develop to their fullest potential. The Healthy Cities movement provides a pathway for upstream thinking.

Family social policies have traditionally taken a "backseat" with politicians in many countries. The United States, with a very different social-political environment, has no comprehensive policy to guide its hundreds of programs for children (Brewer, 1987). It is difficult to expect a country like Russia, grappling with democracy, market reform, and growing inability of its citizens to afford the basics of life to continue this concern for adolescents -- except that it is one of the ways it can better prepare the next generation for responsible roles in society. Gothenburg and Glasgow Healthy Cities, on the other hand, have taken active steps to promote healthy public policies for their citizens. This is commendable considering the financial constraints of most societies and the fact that many policy makers may identify other problems as taking priority.

Currently the indicators of health such as teenage pregnancy rates, maternal mortality, problems of women and the elderly continue to increase. Clearly, family specialists, parents, policymakers -- the society as a whole -- must rally resources and strengths to reduce these inequalities in health and thereby to help people of all ages to develop their skills for responsible roles in society. The circular nature of the problems demand creative and intersectoral approaches which are new concepts for most professionals and policy makers. Over time, the Healthy Cities approach in these cities and others may demonstrate that local participation in health decision making can facilitate upstream thinking in democratic societies and countries that have previously only known totalitarian rule, many of which are now emerging democracies.

Family and community health are mutually dependent. Families rely on communities to support their health, and communities rely on families to produce healthy generations to assume responsible roles in society. Creating supportive environments to assist people of all ages in achieving sexual as well as social and psychological maturity and independence promotes the recognition of the family-community interdependency in health. It is only when all people are viewed as valuable members of society that programs for them can reduce their social inequities and support healthy families and healthy communities.

References

Abortion Report. (1992). Fifth Avenue, NY: The Alan Guttmacher Institute.

Adelson, J. & Doehrman, M. J. (1980). The psychodynamic approach to adolescence. In J. Adelson (Ed.). Handbook of Adolescent Psychology, (pp. 99-116). New York: John Wiley & Sons.

Brewer, G. (1987). The policy process as a perspective for understanding. In E. Zigler, S. L. Kagan, & E. Klugman, (Eds.). Children, families, and government. Cambridge: Cambridge University Press.

Chamberlin, R.W. (1992). Personal Communication. Unpublished.

Draper, R., Curtice, L., Hooper, J. & Goumans, M. (1992). WHO Healthy Cities Project: Review of the First Five Years, (1987-1992). Copenhagen, Denmark: World Health Organization Regional Office for Europe.

Flynn, B. C., Rider, M. S. & Ray, D. W. (1991). Healthy Cities: The Indiana model of community development in public health. Health Education Quarterly. 18(3), 331-347.

Garnick, S. & Short, T. (1985). Utilization of hospital inpatient services by elderly Americans. (DHHS Publication No. PHS 85-3351). Washington, DC: Government Printing Office.

Gurkin, U. (1992, July). Description of the center for reproductive health services. Paper presented at meeting with World Health Organization Consultants, St. Petersburg, Russia.

Indiana State Department of Health. (1990). Indiana Vital Statistics and unpublished data.

Kirichenko, V. (1992, December). The health of childbearing age-women and mortality issues in St. Petersburg. Paper presented at the meeting of the World Health Organization, Consensus Conference, St. Petersburg, Russia.

Teens and Tots at School. (1992, March 11). Indiana Weekly, A Special Publication of the Courier-Journal.

Tsouros, A. D. (Ed.). (1990). World Health Organization Healthy Cities Project: A Project Becomes A Movement. Copenhagen, Denmark: FADL Publishers.

Tusheva, E. T. (1992, December). Overview of health services for mothers and babies. Paper presented at the World Health Organization, Consensus Conference, St. Petersburg, Russia.

U.S. Senate Special Committee on Aging. (1992). Aging America: Trends & projections. Washington, DC: U.S. Government Printing Office.

Wagoner, M. (1992, March). MCH consultation to healthy cities project in St. Petersburg, Russia. Paper presented at meeting with Healthy Cities Project Officer, Copenhagen, Denmark.

WHO & UNICEF. (1978). Primary health care. Geneva, Switzerland: WHO.

WHO. (1986). Ottawa charter for health promotion. Copenhagen, Denmark: WHO Regional Office for Europe.

Gender Issues in Families in the Developing World

Barbara H. Settles

Barbara H. Settles, Ph.D.
Professor of Individual and
Family Studies
University of Delaware

"The well-being of families, the achieving of equal opportunities for women and the sharing of roles by men and women require new perspectives, concepts, patterns of partnership and sharing within families;..."

1994 International Year of the Family. "Building the smallest democracy at the heart of society", pg 17. United Nations, Vienna, 1991.

From the moment that the gender of persons is known, their everyday life, opportunities for choice and life chances are determined. Participation in the family and social context including work, education, wages, and fertility decisions are influenced by the way gender is built into the structure of society. Within families and within social contexts, as well as across nations, the specific activities and expectations that are gender-linked for men and women vary greatly. Frequently women have more of their lives and concerns vested within the family as an institution than do men. The subordination of women to men frequently occurs in varied forms. Even where there exists a rhetoric of equity and fairness, there are different ideas of what constitutes appropriate behaviors and outcomes for girls and boys and then later for men and women. There has been a trend toward egalitarian role preferences in the United States over the last three decades (Thornton, 1989). Nevertheless, gender specialization in marriage, work, and parenthood continues (Thompson & Walker, 1989). The wide differences among other countries, subcultures, classes and communities in gender behavior were not always visible in the past. These differences are more easily perceived when migration, social and economic change, and media exposure bring these varieties of social content in gender roles directly to the attention of ordinary families (Settles, 1994, in press).

The forces of change, choice and communication have permeated every small place and distant land. Families are no longer as isolated and families all over the world recognize that gender roles may be structured in alternative ways. Yet, agents of change often err by extrapolating from the feminist movement in the western developed world to other nations (Nader, 1986). For example, the assumption is sometimes made that nations having subordinate roles for women would best handle new development efforts by channeling resources through the husbands, thus contributing to women's misfortunes in many ways. Blumberg (1988) reviewed the consequences of different approaches to economic development and gender. In many situations, family well-being and nutritional status were lowered by paying husbands instead of the actual workers, the wives. While economists have begun to include the household as a unit of analysis, Becker's "new home economics" has not yet focused attention on what happens in terms of who receives what compensation (Blumberg, 1988). How can we better understand gender, so that new proposals for change and international intervention can identify the unintended consequences of policies on men and women? How can we analyze development policies so that we can address the hidden agendas for promoting gender inequalities?

State of Present Knowledge

Education for women, availability of reliable contraception, lower maternal and infant death and morbidity rates, and employment opportunities in the money economy for both men and women accentuate the changes in gender roles (Keyfitz, 1989). When the technology for fertility control and opportunity for education and waged work are available, women in these settings have more opportunity to be independent in their choice of activities and enjoy a greater role in family decision making. For men the situation is more complex and change is slower. Men who are well educated and who have reliable employment may be able to continue with traditional role arrangements for a longer time. In some polygamous African groups, powerful families can find women who are willing and interested in the trade-offs for traditional arrangements (Adams, 1993). Men who do not have the opportunity to provide for their families on a regular basis and at a sufficient level may be pressed out of their households or may never marry at all. Women and children then increasingly constitute the family, no matter what the traditional definition of family may have been or what continues to be the legally preferred family form (Folbre, 1991). When people are faced with gender role choices they often see the changes as progress or as the destruction of their culture and lives.

Many aspects of the research and theory addressing gender issues have been highly politicized and may not be helpful for analyzing family, gender and development. Osmond and Thorne (1993) note that the choices of theory used to examine these issues do impact on what research and intervention is done. For example, in the United States medical research on cancer was limited primarily to men for many years because of the "difficulty" of dealing with the hormonal differences in women.

The tendency among family scholars to support stable elements in family life and to be uneasy about change and perceived instability has both theoretical and social roots in the development of social science within western traditions. For example, only recently has physical and sexual abuse of children and women in families gained the attention of policy makers and researchers (Straus & Gelles, 1986). The neglect of reports by victims over the years is partially due to the acceptance by social workers and psychologists who interpreted such reports from girls and women as fantasy, not reality. Currently, in some countries, training police forces to handle domestic violence in a more serious way has been successful in reducing that violence. Programs that specifically reduce violence toward children and women within the family and the violence in the larger society are central to gender equality in the long run. Until women's rights are well established, public action to promote women's well-being in the family realm will be problematic.

Exemplary Action on Behalf of Families

In the international arena, examining the connections between gender and the family is difficult. It is challenging to understand many specific cultural differences while at the same time noticing the generic themes resonated across the world. Developing a conceptual understanding of families that is inclusive of many types of families emerging across the world is an important challenge to the family field. It is otherwise difficult to accommodate gender role shifts for these families (Levin & Trost, 1992). Even when countries have similar family policies and legal codes, the issues surrounding the definitions of families and availability of services and support, greater mobility and economic interchange cause difficulties in providing for international legal gender equality (Dumon, 1991).

An important reform would be implementing economic and social development so that individual families do not carry all the transitional costs of such programs. Currently, burdens for development are not equally carried by men and women. Although women have been mentioned in development plans, they are often excluded from management and priority setting functions. The recent inclusion of a family initiative in U.S. A.I.D. programs is a positive sign, but established bureaucracies are difficult to change. It will take some effort to redirect policies in order to do more appropriate, smaller projects that really address gender and the family.

Many barriers are put in the way of families and of women, in particular, in participating in market economies that might benefit them. Pressures and restraints on family and individual migration, labor organization, access to vocational education, and small farm and business capital have restricted families from taking effective action to improve their quality of life. Gender-related economic problems include; the separation of families so that either or both spouses can find work; the employment of women in domestic or unwaged work that separates them from their children and husbands; the growth of the markets for prostitution and labor exploitation of women and children with no outlook for their own family life or personal independence. The continuation of bonding and near slavery conditions in some businesses, and the offshoring of production and jobs from one country to another undercutting wages and benefits, also affects gender roles in families.

While both men and women suffer under situations of extreme poverty and unfulfilled needs that make them vulnerable to exploitation, gendered differences are built into government systems intent on increasing economic activity. The production of women and men outside the wage economy is not included in the economic data keeping used in planning and policy making. An interesting example is from the lace trade in one part of India. The women work long hours producing the lace, but it does not become a product in the economy until men who pick it up by bicycle then sell it. They are in "business" and part of the economy, but the women are not (Mies, 1982). Many development project proposals by women's groups for small business or cooperative ventures are not funded because they are too small and, therefore, cost too much to administer. Women have had no chance to gain experience suitable for managing business. If their venture does not have the potential for scaling up, many funding agencies are unwilling to invest in them. Most of these funders' objections are based on gendered differences in opportunity or stereotypes about women's skills in the nonwage productive sector. Development theory is giving some attention to empowerment and equity approaches to economic and social development and some models and demonstration projects are being launched to explore how families can be included in development work without unwarranted splash-over of gender discrimination (Moser, 1989). Some of the more successful development for families and women's projects from Europe and Canada have emphasized training and support for local cooperatives and community infrastructure building of clean water, sanitation, and community buildings. Management and group building skills, appropriate technology and sustainable agricultural techniques have been successful in delivering equitable development to families.

Looking Ahead

There are many areas in which there are possibilities for exemplary international action to foster economic development on behalf of families without limiting the flexibility of gender roles. In legal codes, relative parity is needed. Legal reform and renewed commitment to the enforcement of international conventions and agreements are needed for gender equality, and for families to be protected from exploitation.

It is not sufficient to address family law and micro level regulation alone. The structure of unequal gender roles runs deep into the macro level economic and political decisions made by multinational companies and national interests. The importance of examining the costs and benefits of economic and political development for differential impacts by gender and consequences for family life needs to be identified and advanced by family experts. A reinvention of the accounting system of costs and benefits requires when costs are shifted from the macro actors, (multinational industries, banks, development agencies, defense alliances, etc.), to the micro actors, (families and individuals), that appropriate compensation be given to those affected by such actions.

In many countries, world financial institutions have required major cuts in public health and education in order to pay for oil related debts of the third world institutions. The costs are directed to poor women and their children while the benefits are funneled to the elites. In the developed countries the costs of downsizing of industries are being born by families. The lowest wages of women's work are becoming the new standard for compensating all labor. It is a myth for men to assume that subordination of women does not have costs to them as well.

Family programs need to be developed and evaluated with sensitivity to gender issues and to avoid stereotyping and inadequate cultural understanding. Among the issues needing immediate attention in the international arena are:

- Adequate fertility and sexually transmitted disease information and technology that is cultural and gender sensitive for both males and females, and available to youth as well as adults.
- Adequate enforcement and information on legal rights available across gender lines.
- Access to education and wages should be gender neutral.
- Research on and development of appropriate gender sensitive programs to identify and address cultural practices and laws that are not in keeping with individual dignity and family integrity, i.e., female circumcision, bride burning, child marriage, domestic spousal violence, physical punishment of children, and exploitation of handicapped or elderly.
- Development of decision making and long term planning education for families that is gender equitable across the whole life course.
- Developing low cost educational and therapeutic approaches to bring family life information to a global audience and that make available to both women and men the opportunities to integrate personal and family well-being while dealing with social change.

Conclusions

Many more family issues that have gender aspects need to be examined. Our task is to be careful not to assume too much and to carefully examine how gender is addressed by various interventions. Since gender roles are culture-based and are currently changing world wide, there continues to be great resistance from special interest groups. The powerful groups in control of corporations, governments and religious institutions have often seen these changes as attacking their power base and have resisted change. To date women have been the primary beneficiaries of gender role changes, but some men are now beginning to see benefits in more flexible roles as well. Give a person the ability to read and acquire information, create a base of information and she (or he) will use it to gain more personal control and decision making about her (his) own future. Strong families can not be built on a foundation of the subordination of anyone by coercion, violence, or ignorance. More freedom and less limitation by gender are the promises of today's trends, but informed efforts will be needed to accomplish these potential goals. However, families and the individuals within them, will still want some differentiation of roles and responsibilities on the basis of skill, interest and personal capacity.

References

Adams, B. (1993, June). <u>Bridewealth and Polygyny</u>. Paper presented at the International Sociological Association Committee on Family Research XXIX Seminar on Rapid Social Change, Palanga, Lithuania.

Blumberg, R. L. (1988). Income under female versus male control. <u>Journal of Family Issues</u>, <u>19</u>(1), 51-84.

Dumon, W. (1991). <u>Families and policies: Evolution and trend in 1989-1990</u>. Brussels, Belgium: European Observatory on National Family Policies, Commission of the European Communities.

Folbre, N. (1991). Women on their own: Global patterns of female headship. In R. Gallin & A. Ferguson (Eds.), <u>The Women and International Development Annual 2</u>, pp. 89-126. Boulder, CO: Westview Press.

Keyfitz, N. (1989, September). The growing human population. <u>Scientific American</u>, pp. 119-126.

Levin, I., & Trost, J. (1992). Understanding the concept of family. <u>Family Relations</u>, <u>52</u>(3), 348-351.

Mies, M. (1982). The dynamics of the sexual division of labor and the integration of rural women into the world market. In L. Beneria (Ed.) <u>Women in Development: The Sexual Division of Labor in Rural Societies</u>, pp. 1-28. New York: Praeger Publishing, C.B.S.

Moser, C. O. (1989). Gender planning in the third world: Meeting practical and strategic gender needs. <u>World Development</u>, <u>17</u>(11), 1799-1825.

Nader, L. (1986). The subordination of women in comparative perspective. <u>Urban Anthropology</u>, <u>15</u>(3-4), 377-397.

Osmond, M. W., & Thorne, B. (1993). Feminist theories: The social construction of gender in families and society. In P. G. Boss, W. J. Doherty, R. LaRossa, W. R. Schumm, & S. K. Steinmetz (Eds.), <u>Sourcebook of Family Theories and Methods: A Contextual Approach</u>, pp. 591-623. New York: Plenum Press.

Settles, B. H. (1994, in press). The illusion of stability in family life: The reality of change and mobility. In B. H. Settles, D. Hanks, III, & M. B. Sussman (Eds.), Families on the Move. <u>Marriage and Family Review</u>, <u>19</u>(1-4). Haworth Press.

Straus, M. A., & Gelles, R. J. (1986). Societal change and change in family violence from 1975 to 1885 as revealed by two national surveys. <u>Journal of Marriage and the Family</u>, <u>48</u>(3), 465-479.

Thompson, L., & Walker, A. J. (1989). Gender in families: Women and men in marriage, work, and parenthood. <u>Journal of Marriage and the Family</u>, <u>51</u>(4), 845-871.

Thornton, A. (1989). Changing attitudes toward family issues in the United States. <u>Journal of Marriage and the Family</u>, <u>51</u>(4), 873-893.

Husbands, Wives & Partners: Definitions of Marriage and divorce in Law & Practice

The Honorable Justice Alastair Nicholson

The Hon. Justice Alastair Nicholson AO RFD
Chief Justice, Family Court of Australia

"Family law is a most pervasive form of family policy and varies according to the legal system and policies adopted in different countries."

1994 International Year of the Family. "Building the smallest democracy at the heart of society", pg 20. United Nations, Vienna, 1991.

The traditional common law definition of marriage as a voluntary union for life of one man and one woman to the exclusion of all others seems far removed from the reality of many Western contemporary societies. Demographic characteristics of countries such as the U.K., U.S.A., Australia and Canada illustrate high divorce and non-marital cohabitation rates, and increasing extra nuptial birthrates. In addition, calls are frequently made by the gay and lesbian communities for formal recognition of same sex relationships. This may take the form of a registered partnership conveying specific rights and duties such as that found in some jurisdictions of the United States or the equivalent of heterosexual marriage introduced in Denmark in 1989.

Despite the diversity of family forms, many jurisdictions continue to give priority to partners in de jure marriages in areas such as pension entitlement, accommodation, intra-partner financial arrangements on separation and death, and adoption. This may be partially a matter of pragmatics, as recorded marriages are easy to prove and de facto relationships come to attain the trappings of marriage only upon the affluxion of time. It may also be the remnant of government policy, which has equated formal marriage with societal stability, and sees the welfare of children as being more likely to be advanced in a traditional family environment than in an informal relationship (Giesen, 1993). However, such preferences are now frequently considered to be discriminatory in nature, and many are prohibited in many Australian States under antidiscrimination laws.

State of Present Knowledge

AUSTRALIAN STATISTICS

Australia has an average marriage rate of 6.6 per 1,000 and a divorce rate of 11 per 1,000 married couples. The duration-specific rate of marriages ending in divorce is 36.1 and remarriages are slightly more likely than first marriages to end in divorce. The trend is for men and women to delay marriage, and currently the average ages at first marriage are 26.7 years for men and 24.5 years for women (Australian Bureau of Statistics, 1991). Put another way, in the four years between 1987 and 1991, the percentage of women who had married by the age of 25 dropped from 57 per cent to 47 per cent and was lower than at any time since the peak of the 1930s depression when the state of the economy discouraged thoughts of marriage.

Statistics such as these have encouraged demographers to query whether a delay in marrying may in fact convert into a decision not to marry at all, and are predicting that about 22 per cent of women will not have married by age 35 at the end of this decade (McDonald, 1991). The average duration of Australian marriages which end in divorce is currently 7 to 8 years between marriage and separation, but about one in five are of less than five years duration. Two-thirds of these marriages have dependent children at the time of the divorce.

Single-parent families represent 14 per cent of all families containing dependent children in Australia, and 90 per cent of these are mother-headed. As in other similar countries, the rate of poverty among these families is particularly high. The ex-nuptial birth rate is currently 24 per cent, but in nearly three-quarters of these births the name of the biological father appears on the birth certificate, suggesting the existence of more than a transitory relationship. The incidence and rate of break down of de facto relationships is obviously difficult to assess, but 6 per cent of couples are estimated to be living in de facto relationships at any one time.

Although the current rate of marriage has declined somewhat since the 1960s, its incidence is still historically high. Formal marriage was not a widespread phenomenon in pre-industrialized 18th and 19th century Anglo-Saxon societies. In the immediate post-World War Two decades an unprecedented proportion of the adult population married. These high rates themselves fuelled the increases in marital separation which became increasingly apparent in the 1960s and which in turn precipitated the wide-spread - and largely successful - call for fundamental divorce law reform which is common to all Western societies.

JURISDICTIONAL ISSUES AND ACTION

Marriage and divorce laws in Australia are constitutionally the responsibility of the Federal government. This avoids the problems of fragmented jurisdiction such as are found in the U.S.A. and Canada, and eliminates the need for border hopping or forum shopping. The Marriage Act (inter alia) specifies requirements for a valid marriage ceremony, the minimum marriageable ages and enumerates circumstances in which marriages are null and void.

Despite the involvement of the Federal government in marriage and divorce, until recently proceedings involving the custody, guardianship, visitation and support of ex-nuptial children were the province of State laws and courts. This resulted in difficulties related to inconsistent approaches and was resolved by the States relinquishing their powers to the Commonwealth between 1986 and 1989. Even so, adoption applications, care proceedings and juvenile justice are still the responsibility of the States.

Legislation in relation to partners' rights and entitlements at the termination of de facto marriages also, for constitutional reasons, emanates, if at all, from the States. The varying views of the necessity for specific legislation, fuelled by concerns that to give rights to de facto partners would in some way denigrate the status of formal marriage, has produced various legislative responses in Australia. Another equally vehement response has come from de facto couples who have deliberately eschewed marriage and the responsibilities it imposes (New South Wales Law Reform Commission, 1983). They object to having an equivalent status foisted upon them after they have cohabited for a particular, statutorily determined, period of time.

New South Wales passed its De Facto Relationships Act in 1984 and defined such a relationship as one between members of the opposite sex, having a minimum duration of two years or resulting in the birth of a child. The Act recognized appropriately drafted separation agreements between de facto couples and provided for property relief on identical grounds to that allowed for married couples under the Family Law Act.

STATUTORY FRAMEWORKS FOR DIVORCE

The Family Law Act came into operation in early 1976. It brought an end to the largely fault-based provisions of the previous legislation and allowed divorce to be granted on the sole ground of irretrievable breakdown of the marriage as proved by a minimum separation period of 12 months. This distinguishes it from the English approach, which still requires irretrievable breakdown to be proved by the establish-ment of at least one of five factual grounds, which include desertion, adultery, or two or five years separation.

Similar changes to those in Australia have taken place in neighboring New Zealand. In 1980, the New Zealand Family Proceedings Act introduced irreconcilable breakdown as the basis for dissolution. In 1985, an amendment clarified the require-ment that the parties must have lived apart for two years immediately prior to the filing of the necessary application.

In Australia, separation may occur where the spouses continue to live under the same roof, although in such cases corroborative evidence is usually required to prove that the marital relationship has in fact ended. Where there are no children of the marriage the divorce may be granted on the papers, otherwise a brief court hearing is required at which the judge or registrar will require proof of the marriage and separation period and will inquire about the arrangements made for the children. The decree absolute, which is normally granted one month after the decree nisi, and which allows the parties to re-marry, may be adjourned if there is dissatisfaction by the Court with those arrangements. However, this very rarely occurs.

Not surprisingly, divorces are very rarely contested and they can be granted against the wishes of a party, provided the 12 month separation period has elapsed. It is more common for women than men to initiate divorce proceedings, and it is more common also for women to initiate the separation. However, men are more likely than women to re-marry, and women are more likely to be financially disadvantaged by the marriage breakdown than men, particularly where they have the care of dependent children as is usually the case (Funder et al., 1993).

Fault based divorce had been roundly criticized in the years immediately preceding the passage of the Family Law Act. As in other countries, objections were raised at the expense and indignity of hearings, there were allegations that evidence was manufactured in order to obtain the necessary outcome and there was considerable cynicism at the ability of judges to determine the real truth of a marriage breakdown in the forum provided (Enderby, 1975). Indications that many couples withheld proceedings, despite being separated for long periods of time, were provided by the sharp increase in divorce applications in 1976. In that year over 60,000 divorces were granted, whereas for the past decade the average annual figure has been between 40,000 and 45,000.

OTHER FAMILY MATTERS

In addition to the introduction of no fault divorce, the Family Law Act established the Family Court of Australia which determines divorce, disputes over matrimonial property, some child and spousal maintenance, domestic violence restraining orders and the custody, guardianship, access and welfare of children. It also has a broad jurisdiction over the welfare of children (Nicholson, 1993). Less than 6 per cent of all divorcing couples litigate their disputes before a judge and the Family Court provides a number of opportunities for settlement, either via conciliation counselling or property conferences. Court counsellors and legally trained registrars are part of the Court staff.

It is obvious that neither marriage nor divorce is a purely private institution, although, as Glendon (1977) has remarked, the State has withdrawn from the formation and dissolution of marriage to emphasize the economic and child-related aspects of marriage breakdown. This is nowhere more apparent than in the area of child support. The State's involvement in the payment of such support from the passage of the Family Law Act until the late 1980s was characterized by increasingly large amounts of public money being directed towards the children of separated parents. Although the individual amounts were far from generous, the magnitude of family breakdown, the non-compliance with court orders and in many instances the complete absence of such orders, resulted in budget blow outs, and resentment by ordinary taxpayers paying, in effect, for other people's children through the allocation of public funds.

The response was similar to that in many American states; the introduction of a Child Support Scheme. In Australia's case, this is administered by the Taxation Office, involves administrative assessment by that office and the elimination of the courts in the process. Although dogged by administrative difficulties and criticized by payers and payees alike, the Scheme has radically altered the role of the State in child support and has focused attention on the financial capacity of the parents themselves, whose responsibility is seen as the primary one.

Looking Ahead

Despite community concern, particularly about the welfare of children, it is apparent that high rates of marriage breakdown will continue to be a feature of life in societies such as Australia. The reasons for this are several and are related to increased secularization, higher attachment to the paid workforce by married women, smaller family size and an emphasis on autonomy. There are increasing calls for greater relationship education programs in schools, as all too often the expectations men and women have of marriage are unrealistic, and neither marriage counsellors nor Courts or other agencies are able to assist many relationships by the time the parties seek any form of help.

Regardless of these factors, the research continues to show that spouses rarely separate easily, and that 'easy' divorce laws do not, in themselves, encourage separation but largely reflect community attitudes. The interface between community attitudes and personal decision-making will continue to influence families and laws.

References

Funder, K., Harrison, M. & Weston, M. (1993). Settling down: Pathways of parents after divorce. Melbourne: Australian Institute of Family Studies.

Giesen, D. (1993). Non-marital relationships including same-sex relationships. Paper presented to the First World Congress on Family Law and Children's Rights (to be published as proceedings).

Glendon, M. (1977). State, law and family: Family law in transition in the United States and Western Europe. New York: North Holland Publishing Co.

McDonald, P. (1991). The shift away from marriage among young Australians. 30 Family Matters, 50.

Nicholson, A. (1993). The medical treatment of minors and intellectually disabled persons - United Nations Convention on the Rights of the Child, Article 23. Paper presented to the First World Congress on Family Law and Children's Rights (to be published as proceedings).

Aging in the Multigenerational Family System

Karen Altergott

Karen Altergott, Ph.D.
Associate Professor of Family
Studies, Purdue University

Demographic, economic, societal and cultural environments are changing interactively, placing the aging family member on the crest of a wave of social transformation. Within an historically unprecedented demographic situation, families face realities of aging and develop innovations in response to challenges. Families operating in vastly different societies and with different kin structures share common realities. Common changes around the world include longer lives and lower fertility, and therefore more opportunity for intergenerational interdependence. At the same time, there are growing needs for formal organization supports for older family members, and more governmental policies that consider the multigenerational family.

The first of these commonalities involves predictable aging, rather than early demise. Longer life, durable intra- and intergenerational relationships, four and five multigenerational lineages are successes of the 20th century. It is only in recent years that most of us can anticipate living to age 65 in the U.S. Even in countries with historically low life expectancy at birth, the length of life is rising. The second of these commonalities involves the necessary transactions between families and societies. Through the availability of services, distribution of public goods through policy, and development of appropriate programs through organizational innovation, the societies around the world either support or hinder the functioning of the multigenerational families. These transactions take many different forms across societies.

State of Present Knowledge

A sizable portion of the world's population is likely to be 65 and older in the next century, a fact that is neither positive or negative in itself. As more adults survive into old age and fewer children are born into the populations around the world, the population structure 'ages'. Alternatively, if fertility remains high while the death rate is unchanged, rapid population growth occurs. Either demographic future has challenges. Currently, the continued demographic aging of the world's populations is considered most likely. In Western nations, the increase in the percentage of those 65 and older from 2-4% to 10-12% took 100 years (Cowgill, 1981), but in the developing world, the population structures are changing much more rapidly (U.S. Bureau of the Census, 1992).

Although aging of populations is common, so is the increasing variety of multigenerational family structures within nations. Every nation contains families that are verticalized (few in each generation but many generations), age-condensed (several generations of early childbearing); and, substitutional (roles emptied through death or low fertility are refilled with fictive or distant kin) (Burton & Dilworth-Anderson, 1991). And, some elders in each society reach old age with no living child. Of those who live alone in the U.S., one-fourth of elderly whites and one-third of elderly blacks have no living children and some have neither sibling or spouse (U.S. Senate Special Committee on Aging, 1991). The patterns of multigenerationality vary widely because each kin group has its own experience of life expectancies, births, and deaths. Nevertheless, multigenerational family structures are increasingly common throughout the world.

Given the aging of populations and increasingly complex and diverse kin groups, the strengths and challenges of multigenerationality emerges as a global family issue. The existing research emphasizes the challenges. For example, problems associated

"Multigenerational families in some societies are ahead of us. [U.S.] dealing with the future we are just beginning to perceive ... we need research, education and service [and policy] on aging in the multigenerational family."

47

with parent care are often described, and this is an increasingly common balancing act for adult generations. One generational exploration has calculated the ratio of those 80 and older (representing parents possibly needing care) to those 50-64 (representing offspring who may have a dependent parent). Sweden now has the highest ratio (57:100), and Japan is predicted to have the highest ratio in 2025 (91:100). Most industrialized nations now have a ratio at 20 or higher. In comparison, developing nations have a ratio of 15 or less, but in the next thirty or forty years, this ratio could rapidly rise to 48 (U.S. Bureau of the Census, 1992). It should be remembered that the existence of older family members does not necessarily mean dependency. While there are increases in limitations of activity with aging, fully 40% of those 85 and older and 60% of those 65 and older and living in the community in the U.S. are not limited in basic activities (Kinsella, 1988).

Strengths of the long-lived adults ought not be ignored. The presence of older kin to help care for offspring often serves the new parent and the youngest generation of a family. Resources of housing and money flow through generational linkages based on need. The older generation as often provides, as it receives the benefits of multigenerationality. In many societies, the oldest generation offers resources of many kinds to their younger family members. This may include land or inheritance or help in daily life. The interdependence of generations rather than the dependence of the old is the most likely family reality. The role of older people in multigenerational systems in the West involves giving and receiving. American elders often give financial support to offspring to buy houses, make major purchases, and for other purposes. In 1990, 3.2 million grandchildren lived in households maintained by grandparents in the U.S.. Services are provided, such as childcare to grandchildren even across households. Two to three million children are watched by grandparents on a routine basis (U.S. Bureau of the Census, 1990), and this is more common in other parts of the world.

Geographic dispersion or concentration of kin affects the interdependencies of the multigenerational family worldwide. Shanas, working with an international team (Townsend, Weddervurn, Friis, Milhaj and Stehouwer) contributed to the understanding of the dispersion and interaction of kin in Denmark, Britain and the U.S., where Shanas repeatedly found that about 80% older people who were parents (or about 60% of older people in general) were likely to be located near at least one of their children and interacted often. This pattern remains in the U.S., where 57% of those over 65 who live alone lived near one of their children in 1990 (U.S. Senate Special Committee on Aging, 1991). However, the economy and labor force, housing and space resources operate to spread family members in some kin groups over larger spaces. Some elders live far from kin. In Cairo, an apartment in the suburbs can effectively reduce access to parents in a more central neighborhood, due to transportation challenges (Rugh, 1984). In other national settings, young adults are migrating internationally to achieve labor market goals or to meet basic economic needs.

The increase in older generations should be seen in the context of lower numbers of children and youth depending on family care. Many countries, such as Thailand, China, Costa Rica, will have fewer dependent youth in the multigenerational family at the time when potentially-dependent older relatives become more numerous (Kinsella, 1988). This new family structure of needs requires reorganizing systems of multigenerational care.

This brings us to the second set of changes in the societies around the world: what are the changing policies toward the multigenerational family and how are services and programs sustaining the interdependencies within the family? Older people survive, families exist for most older people, and the community context is more or less supportive. But no society in the past has had vast numbers of adults survive to old age and to very old age. No patterns from the past can serve multigenerational families now. All around the world families are inventing strategies and coping with new care needs. Demographic trends are neither negative or positive in themselves, but they reflect a need to reconsider intergenerational interdependencies in families and communities. The newness of the demographic situation, the new expectations of families and the variable responsiveness of nations and communities creates a sense of uncertainty around the world about aging and the family.

The story of aging within multigenerational families is related to modernization, the economic condition of nations, as well as to developments in public policy and social welfare practices. Access to economic resources, housing, and health care are most obviously beyond the control of individuals in societies with institutionalized retirement (Nusberg, 1982). When economic productivity or accumulated resources in retirement are high for older people, intergenerational interdependence is likely. The lack of resources, pension or productivity on the older person's part may lead to reliance on offspring or to serious deprivation. The situation of older people is directly linked to the larger economy and when there is economic crisis, older people may experience dramatic losses. The availability of either pensions, opportunities to work or sufficient resources in the kin network to support nonemployed members are important economic conditions for multigenerational families.

Exemplary Action on Behalf of Families

Public programs that support older family members ought to be considered under the rubric of family policy, since in outcome, they support the interdependent and multigenerational family. Policies for older people regarding economic well-being, access to health care, housing and social services are vital to multigenerational family well-being. In this essay, just a few examples of policies and programs that support the multigenerational family through providing for older generations are considered.

Countries vary a great deal in terms of how much of pre-retirement income is replaced by the public pension. Older people in Sweden receive relatively high income replacement, while other countries with pension plans that are not yet mature do not provide much economic security in retirement (Altergott & Duncan, 1988). Older workers around the world are concentrated first in agriculture and second in manufacturing (Kinsella, 1988). Issues of pensions are linked to need for the worker's productivity and the worker's need to maintain the economic status of the family. The economy, policy and national agenda setting shapes the multigenerational family by providing opportunities to work and opportunities to retire with sufficient economic resources. Facilitating retirement through adequate public and private pensions benefits the family through allowing older people to remain economically interdependent rather than dependent on younger kin.

Likewise, variations in health care cost and provision make an enormous difference for all generations of the multigenerational family. Universal programs that support health care in places like Canada, Sweden and the United Kingdom meet the needs of all generations. In some countries, separate funding for exceptional medical expenses such as nursing home care or other extraordinary care to citizens of any age allow families to seek appropriate care at the time it is needed (Kane & Kane, 1985).

Economic stability through pensions that are sufficient to maintain an adequate lifestyle and health care coverage that prevents illness from destroying that lifestyle are two policies that are basic to the multigenerational family. Younger generations bankrupt themselves, physically, economically and in terms of time, trying to make up for the lack of support for health care to older members. This becomes difficult when the population of older parents is at an historically unprecedented level and when adult offspring face other demands and limits to their own capacity to provide. Health care costs in most industrialized nations are handled either through a combination of public and private plans, or through public systems of care. In the U.S., only those in poverty (regardless of age) and those over a certain age receive the benefits of public health insurance in 1993. How this will change is not now clear. Only if those developing policies recognize the substantial benefit to all generations of providing health care needs of any generation can we hope to have a family health care policy. Health care costs are too variable across families, and insurance against risk shared across all of our families may prove to be the best option.

Social care that supplements or replaces family care also benefits multiple generations of the family. Whether sons, as in India and Japan, or daughters, as in the U.S. and Nigeria, are considered more responsible, whether filial piety, as in East Asia, or the norm of filial responsibility, as in Northern Europe, is a core value, families provide the bulk of the care to older parents. The pattern of help exchanged within and across households is repeated for nation after nation. Exemplary programs build on this reality, supplement and relieve family burdens without destroying the family bonds (Nusberg, 1984). Support to the family providing care, rather than transferring new and increasingly care tasks to the family ought to be considered. In some nations, extensive and complex medical care can be provided in home environments by family members. The strain this produces, and related health risks, productivity losses and individual and family disruptions, can be increased or decreased depending upon the type of policies and programs surrounding home medical care.

Looking Ahead

Whether the future of the multigenerational family will be absorption in meeting the needs of older family members or whether the active, familial interdependencies among generations will be sustained depends on supportive social action by nations and innovations within our communities. Families prefer and usually achieve interdependence, but some situations are beyond the capacity of families. The future holds many such situations.

As the population ages, a higher proportion of kin groups will contain one or more generations of adults aged 65 and older. As the number of elders increases and the number of adult offspring is reduced within a family system, interdependencies are expected to change in several ways:

1) there will be a reduction of total familial resources available to each older person;
2) resources will be distributed more on principles of need than on generational position;
3) those with larger numbers of offspring or many surviving generations will be more involved in both giving and receiving resources, other things being equal;
4) increasing need of any one generation will lead to mobility of one generation towards another;
5) the adequacy of societal support through public pensions, social programs and health care provision will influence the well-being of the entire multigenerational family as well as the well-being of the individual older person.

The future requires a rapid increase in understanding of multigenerational families and age diversity of our societies among researchers, policy makers and educators. All around the world, researchers are discovering more about aging. Biologists and medical researchers are discovering ways to increase not only life expectancy but active life expectancy. Yet the number of years of independent functioning and survival is increasing even faster than predicted. Social and psychological researchers are documenting the interdependencies, the strengths as well as the losses associated with aging. Yet families and those who serve families have developed countless innovative strategies and benefited from many strengths of the multigenerational family that we have not measured or counted. And educators, who eagerly prepare new cohorts of students to serve children, are just becoming aware of the need to serve all generations of the world's families. Too few programs, motivations and resources are pulling people toward this vital area of family service. The future will be as bright or bleak as we make it. Multigenerational families in many societies are ahead of us, dealing with the future we are just beginning to perceive. To create a supportive future for families, we need research, education and service on aging in the multigenerational family.

References

Altergott, K. & Duncan, S. (1988). National context and daily life in later life: Comparative perspectives, pp. 229-249. Ed. by K. Altergott. Newbury Park, CA: Sage Publications.

Burton, L., & Dilworth-Anderson, P. (1991). The intergenerational family roles of aged Black Americans. Marriage and Family Review, Vol. 15, No. 1/2:311-330.

Cowgill, D. (1981). Aging in comparative cultural perspective. Mid-American Review of Sociology, Vol. 6, 2:1-28.

Kane, R., & Kane, R. (1985). A will and a way: What the United States can learn from Canada about caring for the elderly. New York: Columbia University Press.

Kinsella, K. (1988). Aging in the Third World (International Population Reports Series P-95, No. 79). Washington, DC: Bureau of the Census.

Nusberg, C., with M.J. Gibson & S. Peace. (1984). Innovative aging programs abroad: Implications for the United States. Westport, CT: Greenwood Press.

Rugh, A. (1984). Contemporary family in Egypt. Syracuse: University of Syracuse Press.

Shanas, E., Townsend, P., Wedderburn, D., Friis, H., Milhoj P., & Stehouwer, J. (1968). Old people in three industrial societies. New York: Atherton.

U.S. Bureau of the Census. (1990). Marital status and living arrangement. (Current Population Reports, Series P-20, No. 445). Washington, DC: U.S. Government Printing Office.

U.S. Bureau of the Census. (1992). An aging world II. (International Population Reports, p. 25). Washington, DC: U.S.Bureau of the Census.

U.S. Senate Special Committee on Aging. (1991). Aging American: Trends and projections. Washington, DC: U.S. Senate Special Committee on Aging.

Family Equality and Ethnic Diversity

Harriette Pipes McAdoo

Harriette Pipes McAdoo, Ph.D.
Professor
Michigan State University

"...Families can anchor individuals in traditions and transmit the existing cultural heritage, or more importantly, they can serve as agents of change, reform and cultural innovation."

United Nations Occasional Papers Series, No. 2, 1992. "Family: Forms and Functions", pg 16.

As families all over the world celebrate the International Year of the Family 1994, we need to embrace the diversities that come from the national, ethnic, racial, and cultural groupings of these families and children. Families from countries along the entire development continuum understand the global interdependence that enables us to achieve the many goals of the United Nations. To understand the complexities of these family diversities, one must look beyond the constraints that exist in one locale. Seeing the sum total of all our ancestries and cultures is fundamental to the identities of individuals and the enjoyment of diversity (McAdoo, 1993a).

Families from around the world need to join with those who are like them, and those who are very different from them, in order to celebrate the International Year of the Family. Uniquenesses and similarities are found in all families. Families differ in their values, their cultural histories, in their bonds of kinship and forms of lineages in their patterns of residencies and family values and beliefs. Yet there are many things that all families have in common. These include the love of children, the need to have some ties with their cultural roots and the need for financial and physical security. Families form linkages with those whose cultural backgrounds are similar to their own, creating clusters of beliefs and practices deserving respect. Equality of families means that every family can access the same opportunities to enhance their well-being. This will only be possible when there is an awareness of the inherent importance of culture to the world's families.

Family differences should be celebrated in this International Year of the Family. Diversity all over the world and within our own countries will enrich and add to the increasing awareness of the interdependence of families. In order to have equality between families we need to foster a growing awareness and understanding of both interdependence and diversity to enable us to value all families, regardless of their differences.

As we near the end of one century and move into another, we are experiencing significant changes in the composition of national populations. The future thus requires the acceptance of a growing interdependence upon each other. Individuals from the mainstream families now tend to be older, while those from the ethnic minority families tend to be younger and less educated. Ethnic minority families have made remarkable increases from the 1980 U.S. census to the 1990 U.S. census, but a lack of educational or other opportunities for minority members harms the entire society. Therefore, the need to provide equal opportunities for all citizens is not wholly altruistic, but an act of survival for all of us. It is essential to the well-being of all families to enable ethnic minority families to obtain the education and skill development for their children. That will, in turn, allow them to be productive adults.

One of the many approaches that can be taken to ensure the attainment of equality of all groups is educational in scope. There are many stereotypes and concerns currently held about family groups that need to be addressed. When one ethnic group does not know another well, then there is a tendency to become cautious and refer to those ethnic groups through stereotypes. Preconceptions are held about families when they do not know each other well. When groups learn more about each other and about their culture and history, it is easier to make changes that promote equality for all. When families are thought of realistically, and not as monolithic stereotypes, then it is possible to discover those from all groups which are of like minds (Gordon, 1991). Though individuals and families will find that there are families who differ from them, they will also learn who has similar life goals, and can then work together to attain the type of communities from which everyone benefits.

State of Present Knowledge

FAMILIES FROM DIVERSE GROUPS IN THE UNITED STATES

Families who are of diverse groupings, such as ethnic, racial, or religious minority groups, have had more difficulty obtaining the resources that are necessary to allow them to provide for their family members. Their social status has tended to be lower than average and avenues of accessing resources have often been closed. As a result, they have tended to not move into the mainstream, but have tended to remain closer to their family and ethnic groupings. Families of color face the challenges that are confronting all families today, in greater intensity today than ever in the past. There are several elements that are common to families of color:

- A lack of respect for their cultural uniqueness;
- Family members are often viewed by the wider society in a stereotypical manner that does not allow for an appreciation of differences;
- A general monolithic view of those families exists, without regard for their different socioeconomic, geographical, or religious orientations;
- Extended family patterns become important and often include friends who become fictive kin, as close as family;
- Involvements and frequent interactions with extended family members are common;
- Conflicts occur between families and the wider society, when their children venture out into society confront conflicting values;
- Poverty is widespread because of isolation from economic and social supports of the wider mainstream communities.

Assimilation of ethnic groups into society has long been considered the norm for American society. However, many families of color and ethnicity have faced structural conditions that have prevented their families from being assimilated or even accepted into their own communities. Therefore, these families and communities have felt that it was necessary for them to continue to form protective shields around their children and young adults and to protect them throughout their socio-emotional development. The extended family often provides the traditional support systems for this protection.

The extended family refers to the traditional residential family unit of several generations of a family living together and to those who live in individual residential units. Most families live in separate dwellings, but are involved in patterns of mutual emotional support, frequent visits, and help exchanges. There are often patterns of religious attendance that are supportive of the extended arrangements. These have been cultural patterns that transcend mobility. These patterns of mutual aid have been found to exist at all economic levels, even when the family has been upwardly mobile into middle and higher class.

While extended family support is active for most families, the support and the kin helping arrangements become more activated when the mothers are single, and when families are facing greater stress, or when economic resources are more limited. Socio-economic status and family structure are directly related, because the resources that are available to parents as they raise their children are diminished when mothers are parenting alone. Economic stability of a family is determined to a great extent by the presence of parents who are both working. When the income of the father is removed from the family, the mothers and their children find it more difficult to maintain their economic statuses. Extended family support and help exchanges mediate the impact of stressors on the parent and on the families during stressful times. Key to the extended family arrangements has been the giving and receiving of help from family members in the areas of child care, household tasks, financial support, eating and sleeping arrangements for young children, and giving of advice and mutual support. Fluidity of family boundaries and flexibility of gender roles is a strong component. Inherent in the exchange is reciprocity that requires that the resources of one family unit be kept open and be used by other family units. This can cause tensions at times, but the uncertainties of the future have managed to keep members involved in the exchanges.

The involvement in the extended family support system, the kin help exchanges, the importance of religion in their lives, and the family values that are passed on are related positively to parenting styles and to parents' perceptions of their children. The continued importance of religion as a source of support, and the reliance on extended family members and on friends for support, rather than upon the broader community organizations, ensures that the needed assistance will be available when needed most.

The mutually supportive networks of ethnic families extend beyond the family units into the community. Children are seen as the most vital investment for the future. The entrance of children into the wider world needs special protections. Children from ethnic families of color need to be provided with the educational and job opportunities that will enable them to become productive adults. They need to be provided with the tools that will enable them to succeed and at the same time with the skills that will allow them to transcend the many barriers that arise in their paths. The maintenance of children's self-esteem and their aspirations to succeed must be found in the support of family. In addition, parents and members of the community must continue to protect their children from adverse external influences. Parents need to prepare their children for possible experiences of devaluation when they go beyond the family and community boundaries (Phinney & Rotheram, 1987). As we educate families from the mainstream, there will still be areas where conceptions are still being led by stereotypes (Cross, 1991; Spencer, 1982).

This preparation of children for living in a potentially non-supportive community is called ethnic or racial socialization. This socialization by families gets them ready to live in American communities. This socialization provides children, youth, and young adults with tools that will allow them to function well in the mainstream and in their ethnic communities. Children and parents draw upon the resources of the community as the child goes out to school, to work, and to live in a society that does not value their racial or ethnic group. These approaches result from raising children within communities of color that have been active for a long time. For people of color, it is not just economic adversity that requires them to develop these means of caring for their children.

Rearing children is often rooted in the proverbs that are valued within families. Proverbs refer to beliefs that are measured reflections of a worldview. They are sayings that are passed on from one generation to another to transmit the expressed and unexpressed values of a particular group of people (McAdoo, 1993b). When these wisdoms are repeated over time they become internalized within family members. Family values, expressed in proverbs, are seen as oral traditions that allude to the values in which individuals and families believe. Proverbs have been used to tell stories of the past, to teach messages, and to pass morals to the next generation. These family values guide persons toward acceptable beliefs and goals that have been accepted by the group. We know that some of the values and beliefs most valued by families were self-images, family connectedness, and hard work. Through the use of family values that promote peace and justice, we create opportunities for children of color and consequently for all children. Then, greater equality of families can be attained.

Looking Ahead

Families all around the country and the world are working hard to provide support for their children and their families. All of us are spreading out protective shields to ensure that our children and our families survive. We must ensure that all families have the resources to protect their children. We need to provide the emotional, social, financial, and educational resources to help them reach their potential. This enable all families to nurture the next generation of children.

All of the programs of our communities need to be brought into focus as we strive for equality of opportunities for all of our families, including members of all racial and ethnic groups. Policy approaches, social services programs, and educational services need to be harnessed to promote the equality of opportunity for all families. Public institutions, grandparents and parents, and religious institutions are needed to provide resources and instill hope for all families in the future. Policies and programs must be established that ultimately impact the whole family. All of these resources brought together will enable families to enjoy some equality in the future.

References

Cross, W. (1991). Shades of blackness. Philadelphia: Temple University Press.

Gordon, M. (1978). Nature, class, and ethnicity, pp 67-89. New York: Oxford University Press.

McAdoo, H. (1993a). A nation divided: A melting pot we're not. Ann Arbor News, PA1, A6-7.

McAdoo, H. (Ed.). (1993b). Family ethnicity: Strength in diversity. Newbury Park, CA: Sage.

Phinney, J., & Rotheram, M. (1987). Children's ethnic socialization: Themes and implications. In J. Phinney and M. Rotherman (Eds.), Children's ethnic socialization: Pluralism and development. Newbury Park, CA: Sage.

Spencer, M. (1982). Personal and group identity of Black children: An alternative synthesis. Genetic Psychology Monographs, 106, pp. 59-84.

OTHER RESOURCES

McAdoo, H. (1988). Black families, (2nd ed.). Newbury Park, CA: Sage.

McAdoo, H. (1990). The ethics of research and intervention with ethnic minority parents and their children. In Fisher and Tyron (Ed.), Ethics in applied development psychology, pp. 273-283. Norwood, NJ: Ablex Publishing.

Porter, J. (1989). Developments in research on Black identity and self esteem: 1979-1988. Revue International de Psychologie Sociale, 2(3), pp. 339-353.

Stack, C. (1974). All our kin: Strategies for survival in a Black community. New York: Harper & Row.

Religion and Family in a Global Context

Lina Fong & Daya Sandhu

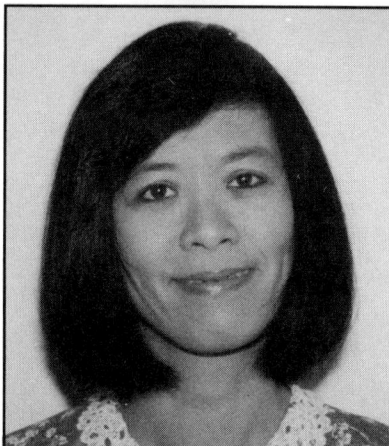

Lina Fong, Ph.D., LCSW
Kent School of Social Work
University of Louisville,KY

Daya Sandhu, Ed.D.
University of Louisville, KY

We live in a global community in which different cultures and world views interact. As the world shrinks, we live increasingly in a context of diverse cultures. We do not have pluralism; we are plural. In the apparent tension existing between a coherent "centeredness" and an openness to "the other," we are all "the other" to someone. Yet we appreciate remaining as we are and "the other" remaining as they are.

Religion reflects the deepest beliefs, vision and experience of reality for peoples of different cultures. Distinctive faith traditions of family units in the broader family of a nation, within One Global Family, are to be respected and appreciated. The growing processes of globalization and ecumenicalization witness the preservation of distinctive faith tradition, amidst the natural development of a shared culture. We need to live in a wider world, but we also need to see our own place in it. It takes a social and psychological project to breathe the spirit of federalism, the federalism of spirit that seems to be one major trend in a shrinking but divergent world. Commitment to one's own faith is not prejudice or a lack of sympathy for other religious positions. Real commitment to faith is secure and belongs to the world of dialogue rather than to the sphere of judgment. This type of commitment combines loyalty to one's tradition with respect and toleration for the traditions of others.

Religion originated from the human belief that we can involve or utilize powers beyond those which we naturally possess. Human consciousness heightens our awareness of our mortality, thus causing a sense of fundamental insecurity. This prompts a quest for postmortem security. According to Cornett (1992), spirituality encompasses the individual's understanding of and response to meaning in life; time and mortality; expectations regarding what, if anything, follows death; and belief or non-belief in a "higher power." Spiritual expression can also be defined as the individual's response to the events in life over which he or she has no control. Crises like disease, natural disasters, and accidents and natural life events as deaths of loved ones constantly make us aware of how little control we have over the world.

Our world of religions can be divided into roughly six main blocks of belief (Smart, 1983). First, the modern West, in North America, Western Europe and Australia, is largely Christian in background, but plural in formal religious systems. Second, the Marxist countries from Eastern Europe to East Asia, are strongly atheist in character, the primary emphasis is on economic change, from Western capitalism to new socialism and finally to communist forms of society. Third, the Islamic crescent, stretching from the shore of Australia through Indonesia, southern Asia, and the Middle East to West Africa, which believes in the infallible Koran, daily acts of prayer, and other unifying practices such as the pilgrimage to Mecca. Fourth, the Old Asia, from India around to Japan, lying outside the Marxist orbit, is predominately Hindu, Buddhist, Confucianist and Taoist. Fifth, the Latin South, from the Rio Grande down to Tierra del Fuego on the farthest point of South America, which is predominantly Catholic, with a number of other religions practiced, like Voodoo in Haiti, Protestantism, Hinduism, and Islam. Sixth, the multitude of smaller societies mainly of the South, and especially throughout Africa and the Pacific, are fostering many new religious forms. There are over ten thousand new African independent churches.

Considering the capacity for love and for a spiritual life close to God in Christianity, the insight and compassion of Buddhism, and the actual reform and efforts toward a better life for ordinary people in Marxism; the main goals and objectives of the differing religions and world views are, after all, not that different. Although many people believe in one absolute faith: in the Bible, the Koran, the Vedas, the Marxist tradition, etc.; the elements and spirit about faith are not that different. Faith has an important place in the Buddha scheme both at the entry upon the Buddha way, and in perseverance in the way. Faith is said to be a factor associated with any karmically wholesome state of consciousness whatsoever, at any stage of the religious life. Faith is also seen in Christianity as a body of beliefs and practices, and as one of the three greatest "theological virtues" (I Corinthian 13:13), that constitute Orthodox Christianity. The trust in and commitment to, aside from intellectual acceptance of the Gospel faith in Christianity, reemphasizes that which is observed in the Torah in Judaism. Iman in the Islam faith describes the believers as those who believe in God and his messenger, they do not doubt, and they strive with their property and persons in God's way. In all these faiths, trust in and commitment to a deity, not only in belief, but also in action, is emphasized.

Central to the shape of traditional faiths, and to the estimate of spiritual power of human beings, are the patterns of religious experience which have been absorbed into human life. The mythical dimension of religious experience provides the food which feeds our sense of identity and our destiny in relation to the unseen world — God or Dharma or the Tao or Nirvana. The doctrinal dimension of religious experience, moreover, provides a source of knowledge of what lies Beyond. Veda is founded ultimately on the visions of early seers and sages. The Bible is founded on the visions of the great prophets and the experiences of the risen Christ. The Koran leads us to the revelatory experiences of the Prophet Mohammed. The enlightenment of the Buddha is at the heart of the message of Buddhism. These religious doctrines are organically related to the respective religious rituals through which we mobilize feelings and act out our symbols. They are related to the value judgments we make and to the moral action that leads us into the realm of ethics.

The purpose of religion is to stress the spiritual life — worship of God, a vision of the goodness of the world, the practice of meditation, a perception of the impermanence of things, and so on. Morality has to be related to such a spiritual vision and life. True peace of spirit lies in transcendental humanism — prizing personal welfare but seeing it in the light of a vision of what is eternal. There is a tension between the divine and human sides of Christ, and between the otherworldly and the worldly side of insight and compassion of Buddhism. Faith helps us to see the immortal dignity of each person. Genuine plurality of beliefs and values in society exists with genuine appreciation and tolerance of differences and commonalities in religious and ideological experiences.

"Religion reflects the deepest beliefs, vision & experience of reality for peoples of different cultures. Distinctive faith traditions of family units in the broader family of a nation, within One Global Family… are to be respected and appreciated."

State of Present Knowledge

RELIGIONS AND FAMILIES

Religions typically and traditionally have been nurtured from and through the basic institution of the family. Families often behaved with religious strategies and goals in mind, and the churches grew because of the initiatives of generations of pious householders. Moreover, communal life was that often centered in the religious settings. People dealt with significant life stages, like birth, marriage, death, etc., in ways established and conditioned by religion.

In the Native American Indian tradition, religion or the spiritual side of man, is perceived to be an integral part of every living thing. The description of "Grandfather" as the "Creator," or "Great Spirit" as the center of most of these religious beliefs illustrates the close connection between religion and family.

In the Christian tradition of the Modern West, the domestic emphasis on spirituality was pronounced in as far back as the Carolinian age and the Victorian times. Puritan spirituality was "true to the kindred points of heaven and home" (Jones, Wainwright & Yarnold, 1986). Home was regarded as a church, and what the preacher is in the pulpit, the same householder is in the house. Early settlers who came to the New Land with the hope for religious freedom, were predominantly imbued with the doctrine of Puritanism, or Reformed Protestantism. Family and church were charged with the responsibility of imparting religious faith to the children who were believed to be born without the fear of God and with original sin. America was founded "under God" and its currencies bear the inscription "in God we trust."

Eastern Christendom sees "the Church as an earthly heaven, in which the heavenly God lives and moves" (Alexander, 1958). The spirituality of the icon also extends beyond the church into the home. In each Orthodox household, there is traditionally an icon corner or shelf. At this shelf, lamps are lit, incense is offered, and the family prayers are said. This too is felt as "heaven on earth" (Jones et al., 1986).

Throughout the past 2000 years, Chinese as well as many other Asian cultures have been principally influenced by the doctrines and philosophies of Confucianism, Taoism, and Buddhism. In these philosophies, from which the family is regarded as the "place" where the most important events in life take place. For example, ancestral worship takes place in the home, rendering the home the center for religious worship (Rutledge, 1992). The Asian family has been a living organism linking generations of ancestors with generations as yet unborn. In the governance under the principles of strict Confucian morality, the reciprocal roles in households are described. The householder is to show affection to his preceptors in act and word and thought, must offer them hospitality, and supply their temporal needs; the religious preceptor is to restrain the householder from evil, exhort him to good, be kindly disposed towards him, teach him what he does not know, correct him when he makes mistakes and reveals to him the way to heaven.

Due to the influence of the Spanish heritage, the majority of Latinos in the world are Roman Catholics. The Hispanic culture emphasizes the primary importance of the family, on personalism and a concern for spiritual values. In the Cuban culture, Santeria tends to promote and strengthen traditional family ties, since the religion models a pantheon of saints and deities that interact as a "sacred family." Orchun is the Santeria saint who is the patron of love, marriage, fertility and gold (Gonzalec-Whippier, 1989).

Early African religion was centered on the concept of a supreme God who created the Earth, and that this Creator had a life force that was present in all things. The worship of ancestors and the spirits existed simultaneously. Ancestors were venerated and deified upon their death, and it was believed that the ancestral spirit stayed with the family as protector. Religion and family were thus inextricably woven. Islam and Christianity did not supplant tribal religious practices, though they clashed in a struggle for the souls in early Africa.

Religions have continued to act as mediating structures between families and the larger society. They have offered a variety of supportive as well as controlling features that many families have found to be helpful. Families and religions share values that help to continue to bring them together, and may, at times, even set them against the tide of prevailing societal values. The values of love, compassion, and self-sacrifice, along with acceptance of and cooperation with others, may set the two institutions apart from the individualistic competitive, achievement-oriented values emphasized in schools, workplaces and governments. Consanguineous, collective ties and cooperation form the basis for group acceptance. Religions and families encourage a strong sense of duty, obligation, and caring for their members.

Religions have continued to play an important role in providing comfort and support to families in times of celebration, e.g., birth, marriage, and in circumstances of crises, such as death and dying, divorce, abortion, and so on. In fact, religions have continued to play an important role in the mental health of individuals and their families as a whole. Faith and optimism gives a strong edge in mental health. Knowing God is always with you in everything you do makes things more certain than if you have to do things all by yourself. Optimism is linked to allowing religion to influence daily life, and the hope it gives that earthly suffering will be rewarded (Courier Journal, 8/23/93).

The code of ethics that religion embodies, along with the norms local religious groups and leaders choose to emphasize from this code, has long served as the basis for social sanctions. It has contributed to family solidarity, and denominations' continuance, through its emphasis on religious endogamy in marriage, the limiting of sexual intercourse to conjugal relations, and high fertility. Religious sanctions have also operated to enforce family conformity. Families often conform to norms because of personal belief, rewarding friendships within the religious body, and possible positions of leadership in the group, as well as the fear of gossip and the cutting of emotional ties as a result of their nonconformity (D'Antonio & Aldous, 1983).

On a more macrolevel, religions have been instrumental in lending support to the oppressed, uplifting them through speaking out for social justice. For African-American and Hispanic-American families, religion has played a central role. Historically, churches and religious leaders support, comfort and build identity to ease the pain of living in a violent and racist society. Martin Luther King sought to exercise the social control function of churches in the interest of nonviolence among his followers in their push for equal rights. As religious leaders engage political and economic leaders in debates over the morality of nuclear war, there may be far-reaching consequences at the family level that we can only now glimpse through the glass darkly (D'Antonio & Aldous, 1983).

In short, religion plays an important role in shaping individuals' and their families' lifestyle and outlook towards life, in impacting directly on government, food, welfare, health, human rights, and justice in countries dominated by the different religions. Many significant events — the remarkable rise of Islamic fundamentalism, the victory of Afghanistan over the Soviet Union, the continuing conflicts in Northern Ireland, Lebanon, Israel, Cyprus, Lebanon, Tibet, Pakistan, Sri Lanka, Yugoslavia - can hardly be appreciated without a deep understanding of the religious views of those involved (Sollod, 1992).

Looking Ahead

We live at a time when the opportunities are unique for seeing the way religion and world views change through the interactions and migration of humanity. Study is beginning to explore how religions react when they experience an extensive diaspora, where adherents live scattered in foreign places and cities; e.g., Hinduism in Fiji and Guyana, Buddhism among Vietnamese in Los Angeles, Chinese world views in Singapore and San Francisco, Islam in Britain and Germany, Zulu religion in the cities of South Africa. Religion itself is deeply affected by social change, and new movements arise and grow from the challenges of change and interaction.

The inquiry into the relationship of family and religion in the global context offers opportunities to explore or test unconventional methods of research — a fact that should make the undertaking all the more attractive and challenging to scholars who are seriously concerned about recovering these fundamentals of human experience in past time (D'Antonio & Aldous, 1983).

As we are stepping gradually into the years of the 21st Century, hopefully by knowing and appreciating our faiths more profoundly, and knowing and appreciating the faiths of others more accurately, we can live ever more fully, as members of One Global Family. Hopefully, spiritually wholesome individuals through their strong spirituality and active faith or religious participation, are more apt to found and sustain strong families in each National Family, and national harmony and international understanding can thereby be promoted to make our One Global Family, a strong, enriched, and enjoyable home for us all on earth.

Our tender wisdom and heartfelt appreciation are called for to comprehend the deep spirituality inherent in interpersonal relationships and in many social, economic, and political movements, that are impacting the lives of individuals and families.

References

Alexander, P.J. (1958). The patriarch Nicephorus of Constantinople. Oxford: Clarendon.

Cornett, C. (1992, March). Toward a more comprehensive personalogy: Integrating a spiritual perspective into social work practice. Social Work, Vol. 37(2)

D'Antonio, W., & Aldous, J. (1983). Families And Religions. Los Angeles, CA: Sage Publications.

Gonzalez-Whippier, M. (1989). Santeria, the religion. New York: Harmony Books.

John Paul II. (1979). The Redemption of Men. Boston, MA: Daughters of St. Paul.

Jones, C., Wainwright, G., & Yarnold, E. (Ed.). (1986). The study of spirituality. New York: Oxford University Press.

Rutledge, P.J. (1992). The Vietnamese Experience. Bloomington, IN: Indiana University Press.

Sollod, R. (1992, March 18). The hollow curriculum - the place of religion and spirituality in society is too often missing. Chronicle on Higher Education.

OTHER RESOURCES

Brandon, S. G. F. (Ed.). (1988). A dictionary of comparative religion. New York: Macmillan Publishing Co.

Kennedy, W. E. (1992, Fall). Diversity in a postmodern context - Association of Professors and Researchers in Religious Education. Religious Education, 87(4).

Lynch & Hanson. (1992). Developing cross-cultural competence. Baltimore, MD: Paul Brookes Publishing Co.

Mohammed, O. N. (1992, Winter). Multiculturalism and religious education. Religious Education, 87(1).

Moran & Vinobskis. (1992). Religion, family, and the life course. MI: University of Michigan Press.

Smart, N. (1983). Worldviews: Cross-cultural explorations of human beliefs. New York: Charles Schribner's Sons.

Transnational Families: Immigrants and Refugees

Daniel F. Detzner

Daniel F. Detzner, Ph.D.
Associate Professor of Family
Social Sciences
University of Minnesota

*"Adaptation to dramatic change is an important universal shared by refugee and immigrant families while they wait in camps, relocation centers, or third world cities...
Transnational families are composed of survivors... not all members thrive in the new environment. Adjustment... depends on the ability of migrants to establish a support network in the host society."*

There are few better examples of the interconnections within the human ecosystem than the multilevel crisis confronting families who are in transit as refugees, migrants, and displaced persons. In 1993, the number of refugees alone exceeded 18 million persons, the largest forced relocation in human history. An estimated 25 million more persons are internally displaced in their own countries as a consequence of war, famine, or ethnic conflicts. Countless others are also on the move in search of food, economic opportunity, or escape from natural disasters. The impact of forced displacement and large scale population disruptions is found in families leaving behind their land, home, extended kin network, neighborhood, community, language, culture, and nation. Every transnational family faces multiple losses, an uncertain future, and economic hardship as they struggle to establish equilibrium in an unfamiliar and sometimes hostile environment.

Adaptation to dramatic change is an important universal shared by refugee and immigrant families while they wait in camps, relocation centers, or third world cities. Some leave because the climate has changed and not enough rain has nurtured the crops as in Sudan, Somalia, and Ethiopia. Others are forced out by ancient ethnic conflicts as in the former Yugoslavia and Soviet Union. Thousands of Vietnamese boat people risked death in small open boats on the high seas to avoid political persecution, fear, and insecurity. Many more Cubans, Haitians, Chinese, and Mexican migrants follow dreams of improved economic circumstances and hope on alien shores they perceive as filled with opportunity.

Families who choose to migrate in an orderly fashion and those who are forced to leave abruptly from dangerous situations confront different challenges in the process of migration. Cambodian, Hmong, and Laotian refugees experienced harrowing escape efforts with forest bandits seeking to rob them, with soldiers in pursuit as they swam across the Mekong river, and with Thai border guards demanding bribes to admit them to overcrowded refugee camps. Following the escape there were years of uncertainty in camps and relocation centers with no assurance an asylum country would provide permanent relocation. Economic migrants may have a somewhat easier passage because they make a choice to leave. However, they confront similar relocation problems as those who were forced to leave in a crisis situation.

State of Present Knowledge

Some members of transnational families come as individuals or unaccompanied minors seeking to establish a base to which other family members can be brought in a more orderly fashion. Others come as family groups or separated parts of multigenerational family systems. Many separated families have members living on more than one continent with some remaining behind in the homeland, some in camps, and others relocated in one or more asylum countries. The gnawing uncertainty about family members who have not been heard from for years is a unique case of ambiguous loss on a large scale that exacerbates the problems of readjustment.

Those who are relocated inevitably confront significant adjustment problems in the host nation including the immediate need for food, shelter, and clothing and longer term needs for language training, work skills, and family assistance services. Beyond the humanitarian support of host governments are acceptance issues from the host populations, their ability to integrate strangers and their willingness to share resources.

In some receiving countries, there are strong pressures to eliminate the immigrant's cultural traditions. Assimilation efforts may include conversion to the predominate religion, changes in hair style, clothing, and presentation of self, the elimination of family or given names, the discouragement of traditional family and religious rituals and prohibiting the immigrant's language. Many natives are hostile to foreigners in their midst and resentful that crisis situations in other countries have somehow become their responsibility. Discrimination in employment, housing, and other areas of life are likely to affect ethnic minority families for several generations after migration. In some cases, refugees become displaced and a perennial political problem for an entire region. The Palestinians, for example, have a third generation experiencing Middle Eastern camps.

The younger generation of refugees often finds it easier to adapt because they are not as well socialized to the traditions, language, history, and place that nurtured the older generation. This creates a situation where families are composed of multigenerational households at different stages of assimilation. This cultural ambiguity can become a recurring arena of conflict within families as elders seek to retain language and traditions while their children and grandchildren bring unconventional values, behaviors, and ideas from the new culture into the household.

Transnational families are composed of survivors. But not all members thrive in the new environment. Adjustment in host countries depends on the ability of migrants to establish a support network in the host society. Family members who have relocated earlier are an important source of informal adjustment support. Formal support services from the larger community are necessary but they threaten pride, established family relationships, and independence. Often formal services are not culturally sensitive, they lack workers with language skills and ethnic knowledge, and they foster misunderstandings. Many host nations assume that the extended family systems of immigrant ethnic groups take care of their own and do not really need long-term support.

The enormous dimensions of the global transnational family problem is best revealed in the basic demographic data gathered annually by the U.S Committee for Refugees for the World Refugee Survey which includes the estimate of 17,556,900 refugees in 1992. This number includes approximately 5.7 million in Africa, 5.6 million in the Middle East, 3.4 million in Europe and North America, 2.3 million in South and Central Asia, 400,000 in East Asia and the Pacific, and 107,000 in Latin America and the Caribbean. An estimated 24 million additional persons are internally displaced within their own countries and technically not subject to the mandates of protection offered by the United Nations High Commissioner for Refugees (UNHCFR). A multi-year drought, starvation, and political persecution have created a nightmare situation in Sudan, where there are currently 5 million internally displaced persons with no place to go. Other countries with significant displaced populations include South Africa (4.1 million), Mozambique (3.5 million), Somalia (2 million), and Bosnia and Hercegovina (1 million +). In addition, there are hundred of thousands of persons living in refugee-like situations such as the 750,000 Palestinians living in Jordan, the 500,000 Iraqis living in Iran, and the 300,000 Burmese living on the northern Thai border. In 1992, the United Nations took the lead in an unprecedented repatriation of more than 2 million Afghans from Pakistan and Iran, 300,000+ Cambodians from Thailand, and 100,000 Somalians returned home from Ethiopia/Eritrea.

Economic migrants account for millions of additional persons in a state of transition due to forces outside of their control. In the United States alone, it is estimated that there are between 200,000 and 500,000 illegal economic migrants each year, mostly from South and Central America. As many as 100,000 Chinese are estimated to arrive in the United States annually, with most having spent a lifetime of family savings to reach these distant shores.

Regardless of the reasons for relocation, whether it is across international borders or within a country, the amount of time in transition, or the ultimate destination, the economic consequences for individuals and families typically include several generations of poverty. Poor language skills, inadequate preparation for economic productivity, and the long-term psychological impact of multiple losses means that it often takes decades for families to reestablish their independence. In many cases, they are leaving behind poverty only to achieve it at another level in a host country. The absolute poverty and lack of resources in some contiguous asylum countries means that desperate subsistence living circumstances confront some escapees. The relative affluence of Western countries means that even the poor have running water, centralized heat, and refrigeration, unthinkable luxuries in the home villages of Africa, Southeast Asia, and Latin America.

We know that families are often shattered by losing their home, extended kin networks, and economic resources in the process of relocation. In many cases, family members have been brutally murdered or raped in the conflict that led to the leaving as in the current Bosnian situation or Cambodia under Pol Pot. Natural disasters, such as the recurring cyclones that annually batter the coast of Bangladesh and India, leave families with total losses including homes, economic resources, a sense of place, and an extended support network. The death and separation of family members means that significant changes in family structure occur. Because important persons or family roles are missing, traditional rituals cannot be performed.

For some individuals, the horrors that have been experienced preceding and during the escape lead to symptoms of post traumatic stress disorder (PTSD) including recurring nightmares and night sweats, paranoia, hyper-alertness, obsessive hatred of the perpetrators, an inability to concentrate, extreme sadness, and clinical depression. There is evidence that PTSD affects not only individuals but every member of the family who are brought back repeatedly to the ultimate moments of horror in their family's history. Adjustment to these symptoms and multiple losses while trying to establish a degree of normalcy in a disrupted world are major issues confronting families in transit.

First asylum and host countries confront difficult issues in the resettlement of displaced persons. Refugees and migrants are viewed everywhere as a burden to the host society. In addition to the immediate financial resources needed for relief, the receiving countries also incur the psychological and political costs of focusing limited resources on a problem not of their own making, while other pressing human needs go unattended. The responsibilities associated with refugee resettlement is one reason why 62 countries have not signed the 1951 United Nations Convention and/or the 1967 Protocol on the status of refugees and why an alarming number of countries who have signed are pushing back escaping refugees and repatriating migrants.

Exemplary Action on Behalf of Families

ASSISTANCE TO MIGRATING FAMILIES

Despite problems with resettlement, Western Europe, North America, and Australia are leaders in the acceptance of refugees from around the world. Although the United States has historically made a place for millions of refugees and economic migrants, it now confronts significant problems accommodating the large numbers seeking economic opportunities or refuge from harms way. Despite ethnic and racial tensions and serious structural economic problems, the United States granted asylum to almost 1.6 million legal migrants between 1975 and 1991. Canada was a distant second with 216,000 settled during this period, and Sweden was third with almost 140,000.

Of all the Western European countries granting asylum, Sweden's exemplary actions indicate a serious commitment to accepting and resettling refugees, especially those streaming out of the former Yugoslavia. Second in Europe only to the much larger Germany, Sweden currently hosts 88,400 refugees. In 1992, Sweden's contribution to international refugee and aid agencies on a per capita basis was second in the world at $13.61, comparing favorably to the United States at $1.24, Japan at $1.12, and Germany at $0.51. Sweden ranked third in the international community in the total dollars contributed to relief organizations with $118 million behind the United States with $317 million, and Japan with $139 million. The ratio of resettled refugees to Sweden's total population ranked first in the world at 1:62, compared to 1:160 in the United States, and 1:782 in Germany. The Swedish Aliens Act is one of the most liberal in the world including refugees fitting the United Nations "well founded fear of persecution" criteria but also war resisters and persons who are unwilling to return to their native lands because of political conditions there. Although Sweden has demonstrated international leadership, there remains considerable controversy within the country concerning their liberal policies, especially from the anti-immigrant New Democracy Party and others who view existing policy as ruinous.

One of the most hopeful cooperative arrangements has occurred in Central America where the presidents of Costa Rica, El Salvador, Guatemala, Honduras, and Nicaragua signed a peace agreement that combined an end to the hostilities, economic development, and the settlement of problems facing displaced persons. With the help of the UNHCR and the United Nations Development Program (UNDP), an International Conference on Central American Refugees (CIREFCA) guaranteed nondiscriminatory handling of refugees, assured them that they could securely return to their homes with dignity, and find productive roles in either their home or host countries. The participation of nongovernmental organizations (NGO) has been crucial to the success of CIREFCA. In no other place have NGOs had such an important role working cooperatively with international organizations on refugee affairs. Although there are many problems to be worked out and long-term hostilities to be overcome, the CIREFCA model is promising for other regions where conflict affects several contiguous nations and where economic development is central to resolution of the conflicts that create displacement.

Looking Ahead

From an ecological perspective, migratory persons experience multiple layers of displacement at the individual, family, local, national, and international levels. Important issues need resolution at all levels if the growing number of migratory people are to be treated humanely. At the international level, the most important questions revolve around the root causes for ethnic conflict, war, famine, and the equitable distribution of increasingly scarce global resources. How can the individual nations or the United Nations prevent these age-old human problems from becoming worse in the future with increased numbers of dispersed families? Do economically developed nations have responsibilities to help poorer nations or do the solutions lie within the third and fourth world nations themselves?

At the national level, many questions revolve around the reception of refugees and migrant peoples in asylum countries. Whose responsibility are these people? Is it an international problem with the United Nations obligated to help the dispossessed? Under what circumstances, if any, does a nation have a right to turn away from their borders people who are leaving because they dislike the political system, or because of famine, or because they seek improved economic opportunities for their families? How many refugees and migrants should each nation take in and help to resettle and how long does the obligation to assist go on before repatriation is encouraged or forced? When refugees and migrants move into a local community what are their obligations for language, job, and survival training? How should unaccompanied minors be handled? What special needs do women, elders, children, and men have as they attempt to adjust and what can each of them contribute to the well-being of the extended family system?

At the family level, what are the roles of the family system in the resettlement process? How can families maintain cultural and family traditions in a new environment while adapting to new realities? How much of the new culture should be adopted and what aspects must be rejected for the family to survive as an intact unit? What types of programs are likely to provide families with the help that they most need? Is intergenerational and gender related conflict inevitable in refugee families and what can be done to mediate or resolve these conflicts? What types of ethnic organizations can be established in host countries to promote the well being of families? How much support does a repatriated family need to reestablish itself in its home country and who should provide it?

For individuals the questions often revolve around survival, the family, loss and grief, and a sense of meaning. Because the experiences of men, women, children, and elders are so varied it is likely that the questions they face will differ depending on age, gender, and place within the family system. For adults, the issues include providing a safe environment and the basic necessities of life for themselves and their extended family. How can the ambiguous loss of family members and the symptoms of PTSD be treated in a culturally sensitive manner? What multi-cultural skills will most help individuals cope in a host nation that is so different and indifferent and what can individuals do to maintain some degree of continuity in their lives?

The number of refugees and internally displaced persons has increased dramatically in recent years as the bipolar world begins dissembling and a new multipolar world emerges. Although the migration of peoples can be traced far into human history, the visibility of the problems through cable news networks that span the globe has now brought the problem directly into the living rooms of people living in developed nations. The human misery associated with the migrations of population can no longer be ignored. Yet the responsibility for these problems seems to elude our grasp as we hope that someone else will shoulder the burdens and make a place for these disrupted individuals and families. The answers to the questions posed above are elusive but it is clear that the responsibility lies at each level of the human ecosystem. How these responsibilities are shared and the degree of cooperation that emerges in the near future will determine the quality of life not only for those who are displaced but also for those who remain comfortably at home.

References

Gozdziak, E. (1988). Older refugees in the United States: From dignity to despair, 1-55. Washington, DC: Refugee Policy Group, Center for Policy Analysis and Research on Refugee Issues.

Loescher, G. D., & Scanlan, J.A. (Eds.). (1983). The global refugee problem: U.S. and world response, The Annals of the American Academy of Political and Social Science, 467, 9-201.

Martin, S. F. (1991). Refugee Women, 1-103. London: Zed Books Ltd.

Sluzki, C. (1979). Migration and family conflict, Family Process, 18(4), 379-390.

U.S. Committee for Refugees. (1993). World Refugee Survey, 2-154. Washington, DC: American Council for Nationalities Service.

Family Violence:
Searching the World for Solutions

Richard J. Gelles

Richard J. Gelles, Ph.D.
Professor
University of Rhode Island

People are more likely to be killed and physically assaulted, abused and neglected, and sexually assaulted and molested in their own homes and by other family members, than anywhere else or by anyone else. Family life and the home are thought to be warm, intimate, stress reducing; the place to which people flee for safety. Our desire to idealize family life is partly responsible for a tendency to not either see violence and abuse in families or to condone some of it as being a necessary and important part of raising children, relating to spouses, and conducting other family transactions.

Family violence has been a part of the family throughout its history, not only in American families, but in England, Western Europe, and many other countries and societies around the globe. Violence and abuse occur even in societies that have been thought to have little or no abuse. Hanita Zimrin (personal communication) notes that there was considerable attention paid to physical abuse in Israel after a child was beaten to death on a Kibbutz. Zimrin explains, with some irony, that such a case challenged the notion of the "perfect society" and the "perfect childrearing setting"--the Kibbutz. Similarly, case examples of severe physical abuse in China are now making their way into the Western press. In the closing months of 1992, three Chinese children were killed by their parents and their deaths caused an unusual public debate about a problem barely acknowledged in China before (Providence Journal, 1992). On the one hand, many observers in China see these deaths as barbaric. On the other hand, there is the lingering Confucian notion that children must be absolutely obedient to their parents. This, combined with the single child policy in China and parents' high ambitions placed on their one child, has led to increased concern about the problem of physical abuse.

The costs of family violence are significant and horrifying. Child homicide is the fourth leading cause of death of children in the United States. Battering is the leading cause of injury for women and injuries are a leading cause of death (U.S. Dept. of Health & Human Services, 1991). Parents, and elderly parents in particular, are also victims of violence and abuse, as are siblings. The emotional costs to victims are even more difficult to measure or imagine. Victims of violence and abuse suffer from cognitive, developmental, and emotional problems, are more likely to develop alcohol or substance abuse problems, and are at greater risk for suicide. Although not all victims go on to be violent, abuse experiences do increase the risk that an individual will be violent both in and outside of the home.

"Violence constitutes an abuse of power. It often emerges from the desire to dominate, degrade, subjugate, possess and control others. ..The starting-point is to strengthen the strong and well-functioning aspects of families."

United Nations, Occasional Papers Series, No. 3, 1992. *Family and Crime*

State of Present Knowledge

Gathering information on family violence has proven difficult. Only the United States and Canada have specific legislation that requires the reporting of child abuse and neglect—thus there are no official report data on child or spousal abuse available from other nations. There have been few local, regional, or national surveys conducted on family violence in other countries. Thus, our knowledge about the extent of intimate violence is largely based on clinical case data, anecdotal data, or data compiled by anthropologists.

The anthropologist David Levinson (1981) has examined the records of the Human Relations Area Files at Yale University. Levinson reports that wife beating is the most common and frequent form of family violence—thus confirming the theory that women are generally considered the "most appropriate" victims of intimate violence.

Students of family violence around the world have tried to synthesize the various data that are available and come up with a general statement that explains why violence is common in some societies and rare in others. With regards to child abuse, the anthropologist Jill Korbin (1981) concludes that if children are valued for economic, spiritual, or psychological qualities, they are less likely to be maltreated. Certain children who are perceived to have undesirable qualities are at greatest risk of abuse. Thus illegitimate children, orphans, stepchildren, females, or retarded or deformed children are often at greatest risk of abuse. Some students of the new "one child" policy in the People's Republic of China note that an unintended consequence of the law to limit families to one child has been a rather dramatic increase in female infanticide (Korbin, 1981).

Rebecca and Russell Dobash (1979) found that cultural values about women play a role in the risk of wife abuse. The more women are viewed as property of their mates, the greater the risk of abuse. Historically, Roman husbands could chastise, divorce, or kill their wives. Not only that, but the behaviors for which these punishments were appropriate—adultery, public drunkenness, and attending public games—were the very same behaviors that Roman men engaged in daily (Dobash & Dobash, 1979). Today, women in India are subjected to abuse, including fatal abuse, as part of their husband's demands for more lucrative dowries (Prasad, 1994).

Exemplary Action on Behalf of Families

Perhaps the most important action on behalf of victims of abuse and neglect is to raise public awareness about the extent, consequences, and costs of the various forms of family violence. One mechanism that has been used effectively to both treat child maltreatment and raise public awareness about the abuse and neglect of children is mandatory reporting laws. All fifty states in the United States enacted mandatory reporting laws for child abuse and neglect by the late 1960s. These laws require certain professionals (or in some states, all adults) to report cases of suspected abuse or neglect. When a report comes in, state protective service workers investigate to determine if the family is in need of help or assistance.

Few other nations have yet to adopt mandatory reporting laws, however. And, in the United States and Canada, the laws and the attempt to increase public awareness about child abuse, child sexual abuse, and the abuse of women, are not without controversy. While many in the field of family violence believe that family violence remains an under-reported social problem, others (see for example, Besharov, 1990 & Wexler, 1991) believe that public awareness campaigns and efforts to increase reporting have gone too far in invading the privacy and sanctity of families and have produced "witch hunts" and widespread hysteria regarding family violence. These so-called "witch hunts" have, according to some, produced an unacceptable increase in false or inaccurate reporting of physical and sexual abuse.

Efforts to prevent and treat family violence in the United States and globally have pitted two different philosophies of intervention against one another. First, consider the compassionate approach to family violence. Human service professionals who treat violence and abuse from this perspective approach it with an abundance of human kindness and a non-punitive outlook on intervention. The compassionate philosophy views the abusers as victims themselves. The cause of the abuse may be seen in social and developmental origins, and not in the abuser. Abusers, rather than being seen as cold, cruel monsters, are seen as sad, deprived, and needy human beings. Compassionate intervention involves supporting the abuser and his or her family. Homemaker services, health and child care, and counseling are made available to the abuser and the family.

Second, consider the control model. The control model involves aggressive use of intervention to limit, and if necessary, punish the deviant violent behavior. The control approach places full responsibility for actions with the abuser. Control involves removal of the victimized child from the home, arrest of an abusive husband (or wife), and full criminal prosecution of the offender.

In the area of child maltreatment the control approach is likely to advocate removal of at-risk children and placement in a foster home or institution. The compassionate approach provides the family with social support, such as counseling, food stamps, day care services, etc. There is evidence that compassionate family support programs can be effective, especially if they are implemented as prevention programs prior to the occurrence of abuse and neglect. Pediatrician David Olds and his colleagues (1986) evaluated the effectiveness of a family support program during pregnancy and for the first two years after birth for low-income, unmarried, teenage first-time mothers. Nineteen percent of a sample of poor unmarried teenage girls who received no services during their pregnancy period were reported for subsequent child maltreatment. Of those children of poor, unmarried teenage mothers who were provided with the full compliment of nurse home visits during the mother's pregnancy and for the first two years after birth, 4 percent had confirmed cases of child abuse and neglect reported to the state child protection agency. Another prevention program is the "Healthy Families" program implemented in Hawaii. "Healthy Families" uses lay home visitors to provide supportive services to families at risk of becoming abusive. The program identifies participants by screening hospital births and interviewing new mothers. Services are voluntary and continue until the child is 5 years old.

With regards to family preservation and prevention, here too, controversy arises regarding the most appropriate way to protect children. On the one hand, advocates of family preservation believe that programs that keep children with their biological parents are in the best interests of children and are the most cost-effective means of protecting children at risk of maltreatment. On the other hand, critics argue that family preservation programs are naive and place children at risk of further and possible fatal abuse in the name of cost-efficiency and family values (see Gelles, 1993).

The compassionate approach is less often used to treat and prevent the abuse of women. Shelters can be considered one form of compassionate intervention. The first shelters or refuges for battered women were established in Great Britain in the 1970s. Shelters provide a safe haven for victims as well as a source of social support and social and legal advocacy for victims of wife abuse. A second form of compassionate intervention are batterers' programs. Programs for battering men are modestly effective in reducing the risk of future violence.

Control interventions have been the preferred form of treating and preventing wife abuse in the United States and are being adopted in European countries as well. Legislation that requires police to arrest abusive husbands has also been found to reduce the risk of violence--however arresting husbands appears to be only successful for men who have something to lose by being arrested. Thus, employed and married men are deterred by arrest, while unemployed and unmarried abusers appear to increase their use of violence following their arrest.

By far the most effective national efforts to prevent family violence are those that aim at reducing cultural acceptance of violence, reduce the availability of guns, and move effectively towards reducing gender inequality and increasing the status of women and children in the society. All of the nations in Scandinavia have abolished capital punishment, prohibit corporal punishment in schools, and have enacted laws that prohibit the physical punishment of children. Although we have little rigorous comparative data, it does appear that by reducing the cultural acceptance of violence toward children, these nations have reduced the level of abusive violence in families.

Similarly, although scientific evidence is scant, it appears that the rates of violence toward women do vary by the social status of women. Kersti Yllo (1984), examining the status of woman and wife abuse in the United States, found a curvilinear relationship between patriarchal structure and the rate of wife beating. Rates of wife beating were highest in those states where structural inequality in economic, educational, political, and legal institutions is greatest. As the status of women improves, violence decreases--to a point. In those states where the status of women was highest, the rates of wife beating were also quite high. Yllo concludes that where women's status is low, violence is used to keep them in their place, while when women's status is high, conflict arises out of the change in sex roles and balance of power. Rebecca Morley (1994) studied modernization and wife beating among the Papua in New Guinea and found that modernization and the increase in status and support for women did reduce the rate of wife beating. However, as with Yllo, Morley reports that modernization also may produce new pressures, expectations, and changes that raise the risk of abuse for women. Clearly, there are no simple answers or simple solutions for the enduring problems of wife abuse and family violence.

Looking Ahead

Much remains to be done on behalf of the victims of family violence. Only the United States and a handful of other nations are currently attempting to address the problems of sexual abuse and elder abuse. Only a few nations, such as Sweden, Norway, Finland, and Denmark, have taken concrete steps to reduce the cultural acceptance of violence in general and violence toward children in particular. These countries have abolished capital punishment, banned the use of corporal punishment in schools, regulated the sales and distribution of firearms, enacted legislation that prohibits the use of physical punishment by parents, and have attempted to limit the violent content of television programs and movies. Far too many nations are either still in a state of denial about the extent and seriousness of family violence, or have only moved to the stage where only the most outrageous and lurid cases of violence and abuse are recognized. Much more needs to be done to raise public awareness about the extent, causes, and consequences of family violence. Much more needs to be done to explode the stereotypes and myths that hinder recognition of family violence as a significant social problem and to bring social and cultural resources to bear in both treating and preventing violence and abuse in families. In addition, we are only at the very early stages in research on the causes of family violence as well as evaluating the effectiveness of prevention and treatment programs. Much more research needs to be done if we are to unravel the causes of violence and take the appropriate steps necessary to protect victims and prevent violence and abuse.

Family violence is neither new, it is not confined to only the United States or Western nations, nor is it confined only to poor and minority families. Reducing and ultimately eliminating family violence will require fundamental changes in societies and family life that many people will resist or argue that they could not work. Such steps must include eliminating the norms that legitimize and glorify violence in societies and the family; reducing violence-provoking stress created by structured social, racial, and gender inequality; integrating families into a network of kin and community; changing the sexist character of societies; and breaking the cycle of violence in families. Not making such changes would continue the harmful and deadly tradition of family violence.

References

Besharov, D. (1990). Recognizing child abuse. New York: Free Press.

Dobash, R.E., & Dobash, R. (1979). Violence against wives. New York: Free Press.

Gelles, R.J. (1993, Summer). The doctrine of family reunification: Child protection or risk? The American Professional Society on the Abuse of Children Advisor 6, 9-11.

Korbin, J. (1981). Child abuse and neglect: Cross-cultural perspectives. Berkeley, CA: University of California Press.

Levinson, D. (1981). Physical punishment of children and wifebeating in cross-cultural perspective. Child abuse and neglect, 5, 193-196.

Morley, R. (1993). Wife beating and modernization: The case of Papua New Guinea. Journal of Comparative Family Studies. (In press).

Olds, D.L., Henderson, Jr., C.R., Tatelbaum, R., & Chamberlin, R. (1986). Preventing child abuse and neglect: A randomized trial of nurse home visitation. Pediatrics, 77, 65-78.

Prasad, B.D. (1994). Dowry-related violence: A content analysis of news in selected newspapers. Journal of Comparative Family Studies. (In press).

Providence Journal, December 26, 1992, P. C-3

U.S. Department of Health and Human Services. (1991). Healthy people: National health promotion and disease prevention objectives. Washington, DC: U.S. Government Printing Office.

Wexler, R. (1991). Wounded innocents. Buffalo, NY: Prometheus Press.

Yllo, K. (1984). The impact of structural inequality and sexist family norms on rates of wife-beating. International Journal of Comparative Social Welfare, 1, 67-86.

Family-Centered Contributions to a Peaceful Future

Judith A. Myers-Walls

Judith A. Myers-Walls, Ph.D.
Associate Professor
Purdue University

"...The haunting presence of war, conflict and tension are constant reminders of the importance of peace and of the need for peace education at all levels, including the very basic one, that of the family."

United Nations Occasional Papers Series, No. 1, 1992. *Family Matters*, pg 19.

"War is not healthy for children and other living things." This slogan may be truer now than when it appeared on posters, t-shirts, and bumper stickers almost 30 years ago. Although wars have always threatened life, limb, and property, modern wars have changed the look and feel of that threat—and children and families are in the middle of the bull's eye. UNICEF, the United Nations Children's Emergency Fund, has estimated that 80% of the casualties of today's civil wars, insurrections, border disputes, and ethnic conflicts are women and children.

Another type of modern war seems to have faded into the dimly-lit regions of consciousness for many: nuclear war. Although there has been progress in reducing the threat, as long as nuclear stockpiles exist and anyone wants to have such weapons, the risk of nuclear war due to intentional action, human error, or technological malfunction is real and ever-present.

A peaceful, sustainable future for the world depends on coming to terms with the ravages of war in all of its forms. Families, as the most basic of social institutions, must take leadership in learning and teaching how not to make war, or, more importantly, how to make peace. Social institutions must be structured to allow families to complete this task.

State of Present Knowledge

There are at least four ways that war can enter the lives of children and families and disrupt their growth, development, and relationships. These are living in a war zone, experiencing war from a distance, living with the threat of war or violence, and feeling the economic impact of war and military expenditures.

War zones are places where people suffer and die as a result of aggression, hostility, and harsh conflict. They die as a result of bombs and guns, heartache, fear, and starvation. Several authors have investigated the impact of war on children and families in Cambodia, Iraq, Mozambique, Nicaragua, Beirut, the West Bank, and Chicago's inner city (Bryce, Walker, Kanj, & Ghorayeb, 1988; Garbarino, Kostelny, & Dubrow, 1991; Hoskins, 1992). In all war zones they found terror, dismemberment or disfigurement, loss of family members, dislocation, alienation from a sense of history or meaning, inability to meet basic needs, and chaos. They confirmed that war is truly hell. Their findings in these countries/areas identify several common themes.

Day-to-day routines are shattered in war zones. In Cambodia a policy of de-urbanization separated people from their homes and jobs, while in other countries families are dislocated when they try to escape from the fighting. Schools become military targets, either by design or by accident. There is little or no productive agriculture in times of war, causing food shortages and famine.

People, especially children, are injured and die in war zones. In Mozambique, five out of every six deaths in the war have been children. In Cambodia in 1978 the infant mortality rate was 263 per 1000 births. Orphans are everywhere in these war zones, as are widows and widowers. Accidents with unexploded mines and bombs have a delayed but maiming effect. Injuries and disabilities are often the goals of those who are making the wars, as injuries take more resources than deaths and are more demoralizing to the survivors.

Finally, women and children sometimes help to fight wars. Children in Mozambique were often forced to witness or even participate in the murder of their own parents as an entree into Renamo. Children are the predominant gang members and drug dealers in many cities.

Who survives the horrors of war? Any listing of stress coping strategies provides insight, but one overarching ability seems to make the biggest difference: making sense of the situation and finding meaning and an ideology. Almost any ideology seems to contribute to resilience in a war zone; however, if that ideology includes the dehumanization and demonization of others, it may fuel the fires of hate and conflict. The individual may survive emotionally, but the war intensifies.

People do not have to live in a war zone to feel war's impact. With international travel and immediate news broadcasts, events on the other side of the world have become three-dimensional. Sending people as warriors or as "peacekeeping" troops to a distant place moves the events of a conflict into the living rooms of each country involved. In spite of being far away from the war, individuals in those countries may experience family disruption, economic hardship, and death.

Interviews with U.S. children have shown that, even if they did not have an immediate relative in the Persian Gulf War, they felt afraid, sad, stressed, sick, lonely, and angry and had headaches, nightmares, and suicidal ideation. Preschool teachers in the U.S. reported that four-year-olds did not want to go outside while the war was going on for fear of getting hit by a SCUD missile. Apparently, parents recognized their children's fears, but tended to be unaware of their anger and sadness regarding the war. Although there was not an immediate physical danger presented to these children and other family members left behind, there was clearly an immediate emotional impact, and the long-term effect is unknown.

What happens when military personnel return home after going away to war? It is at that point that the stressors of being in a war zone meet those of sending a family member away to war. Hobfoll and colleagues (1991) recommended that returning soldiers and their families: 1) break major problems into their smaller, component parts; 2) take a helper role with others; 3) seek support—both intimate support and attachment to larger social groups; 4) seek professional help as needed; 5) be allowed latitude in how they cope with problems; and 6) understand the normal components of the coping process.

A more long-term coping strategy calls for reeducation of returning military personnel in two areas. First, the suspicion and hate born of the building of enemy images during war must be reversed. Second, returning combatants need to learn nonviolent conflict resolution to counteract their war training.

A significant body of research in the 1980s addressed the issue of children and families coping with the threat of nuclear war. The first conclusion of the studies was that children were afraid; those as young as four associated even the word "nuclear" with dying and being very, very scared. Stillion and colleagues (1988) studied children in six countries and found nuclear worry highest among U.S., Canadian, and Australian youth. Many authors assumed these children would be filled with despair and hopelessness. As the studies progressed, however, it became evident that being worried about nuclear war was related to better functioning. The nuclear threat is overwhelming and the danger is very real, but admitting the danger allows individuals and families to take action in trying to prevent its occurrence.

Many people believe that war is good for a country's economy. Melman (1982) has called this "guns-create-butter" concept a myth. It is not possible to conduct an economic analysis of military expenditures on the financial well-being of a country in this essay, but others have done the analysis. Those figures challenge the idea that high military expenditures make a country economically healthy. A country in transition after high military expenditures experiences unique problems during the time of conversion, also. For example, the U.S. currently is facing unemployment, defense plant closings, and the reorganization of communities located near bases that are closing, and the countries of the former Soviet Union are struggling to find positions for thousands of former soldiers.

Exemplary Action on Behalf of Families

Many projects have been undertaken to help children and families cope with the effects of living in a war zone. A project in a Cambodian orphanage asks teens who have never been parented to care for the smaller children, allowing for "healing through caring". A Family Tracing Project in Angola sponsored by the Save the Children Foundation of the United Kingdom brings together families who were separated from each other during the war. These projects and others make a difference for those who are reached by them, and each is critical in those countries to help to heal some of the ravages of war. But they are not enough.

If the goal is to reach a sustainable future, projects like those above are comparable to putting band-aids on a patient with massive internal bleeding. Maria Montessori (1972) encouraged the making of peace, instead, and challenged the idea that peace is what occurs at the end of a period of war. She built an analogy: There is a beautiful building holding valuable pieces of art. War is like a fire in that building. After the fire is put out, there may be no further danger of fire, but the art and the building are destroyed, and the smoke and ashes continue to choke those trying to breathe the air. What value is peace if it is seen only as the ultimate and permanent triumph of a destructive war?

Other authors also challenge a negative definition of peace. John Galtung determined that war and violence are based on the values of inequality, injustice, environmental damage, and alienation, and that positive peace, therefore, must be based on nonviolence, economic welfare, social justice, ecological balance, and participation. UNESCO, the United Nations Educational, Scientific, and Cultural Organization, also has represented peace as a process, not an event.

The conclusion is that war must be prevented and that peace is a process, not just the absence of war. What exemplary efforts represent this view? Current efforts fall into these categories: national policies dealing with the military, peace movements and organizations, peace education, and parenting for peace and justice.

Costa Rica has taken a leading role in preventing wars. Although it is a small country, Costa Rica has chosen to have no standing army. There is a saying in that country that, "Happy is the Costa Rican mother who, upon giving birth to a son, knows that he will never be a soldier." This small Central American country has been able to realize the highest literacy rate and some of the strongest social programs of the area by channeling money that might have gone into the military into supporting the health, education, and welfare of its citizens instead.

Many countries have witnessed the growth and development of active peace organizations. These groups attempt to effect social change through the building of public awareness and the facilitation of a change in structures and institutions in the society. Germany's active Green Movement is an example of a group that has achieved some political power. The People's Republic of China has reported an active peace movement, at least before the crackdown on the democracy movement there. These movements bring the issues before the eyes of the citizenry and allow for local and/or national or international initiatives to deal with public policy.

Perhaps the most promising approach to achieving a peaceful future is through peace education, or education for peace as it is often called. Ken Parker, an adult educator from Alberta, Canada, has said, "In continuing education from kindergarten through adult education, all educators are responsible for teaching peace". Montessori (1972) points out that those who make wars have realized the need to include the children (e.g. the Nazi youth organizations in Germany during Hitler's time), and that peacemakers need to do the same.

What does effective peace education include? UNESCO's 18th General Conference in 1974 defined the following components of a peace education program: 1) the equality of rights of all people; 2) maintenance of peace; types of war; discrimination; 3) action to ensure the observance of human rights; 4) economic growth and social development; 5) conservation of natural resources; 6) the preservation of human cultural heritage; and 7) the role of the United Nations in solving such problems. Hicks (1986) has identified the skills of critical thinking, cooperation, empathy, assertiveness, conflict resolution, and political literacy; the attitudes of self-respect, respect for others, ecological concern, open-mindedness, vision, and commitment to justice; and knowledge of conflict, peace, justice, power, gender, race, ecology, and futures as critical components of education for peace.

Where does peace education occur? Several countries have or are incorporating education for peace into public school curricula. Bjerstedt (1988) surveyed the Education Ministries or their equivalent in 140 countries or states on every continent to discover their efforts in peace education. He discovered that European schools were most likely to include peace curricula, and the U.S. was least likely. Most reported that individual school districts or teachers may focus on peace as a subject matter, but that, except in the Netherlands, one part of Australia, and perhaps Finland and Russia, it is not standardized. The study by Stillion and colleagues (1988) reported that one-half to four-fifths of their sample of children from six countries said they had never talked to their teachers about nuclear war. Even peace activists and educators have indicated in interviews that peace education in schools was not a big influence in their lives.

Where do children learn about war and peace? Studies and observations indicate that most children report that television is the most common source of information. However, families, as the primary source of socialization and the first source of education, may be the best place to begin. Are families doing that educational job? Apparently not; half or more of children in the study by Stillion and colleagues (1988) reported never having talked with their parents about nuclear war, either. At the same time, children have said they would consider it helpful to talk with adults about war and peace issues.

When parents do talk about war and peace, what do they say? Studies by this author have found that parents say more about war than about peace, and that they tend to represent war as an activity and peace as a more passive state or condition. Direct communication is not the only way children learn about these issues, however. Other authors state that peace begins by treating children with respect. They recommend positive, supportive discipline and communication strategies.

The combination of direct teaching and conscious child management has been called Parenting for Peace and Justice. This author has listed the components of this approach as social change mechanisms, empathy, respect for self and others, affirmation skills, shared power, nonviolent and creative conflict resolution, celebration of diversity, and examination of life style. The Institute for Peace and Justice in St. Louis, Missouri, U.S.A. (address available) has produced a number of materials following this strategy of parent education.

Looking Ahead

Countries, states, provinces, and school systems need policies to support peace education among children, youth, and adults. Parents need assistance in becoming peace educators for their children. But first, we need to invest resources. Policymakers and parents will want to know what works, so we need to evaluate peace education efforts. Some programs have been evaluated, but mostly with college populations, and usually with programs teaching about war and the nuclear threat. How effective is true education for peace?

A second issue is technology. This world knows a lot about the technology of war and violence. "Smart bombs", nuclear weapons, satellites that can almost read a newspaper on the earth's surface, and automatic handguns are only some of the wonders. Unfortunately only a fraction of the time, money, and brainpower has been spent on the technology of peace and reconciliation. If the inhabitants of this world would like to continue to exist, some of that investment will need to be made. Using Montessori's analogy, we have a beautiful building here—Earth. It is filled with amazing and priceless works of art—people, animals, plants, societies. Let us invest more in fire prevention than in fire fighting; we cannot afford to lose or damage what we have.

References

Bjerstedt, A. (1988). Peace education in different countries. Peace education and debate. (ERIC No. ED334143).

Bryce, J., Walker, N., Kanj, M., & Ghorayeb, F. (1988). Life experiences among low-income mothers in Beirut. Journal of Marriage and the Family, 50(3), 811-819.

Garbarino,J., Kostelny, K., & Dubrow, N. (1991). No place to be a child: Growing up in a war zone. Lexington, MA: Lexington Books.

Hicks, D.W. (1986). Studying peace: The educational rationale. Occasional Paper No.4, Revised Edition. (ERIC No. ED289809).

Hobfoll, S.E., Spielberger, C.D., Breznitz, S., Figley, C., Folkman, S., Lepper-Green, B., Meichenbaum, D., Milgram, N.A., Sandler, I., Sarason, I., & van der Kolk, B. (1991). War-related stress: Addressing the stress of war and other traumatic events. American Psychologist, 46(8), 848-855.

Hoskins, E. (1992). Killing is killing—not kindness. New Statesman and Society, 5 (Jan 17), 12-13.

Melman, S. (1982). Teaching about reversing the arms race. Teachers College Record, 84(1), 38-49.

Montessori, M. Translated by Lane, H.R. (1972). Education and peace. Chicago: Regnery.

Stillion, J.M., Goodrow, H., Klingman, A., Loughlin, M., Morgan, J.D., Sandsberg, S., Walton, M., & Warren, W.G. (1988). Dimensions of the shadow: Children of six nations respond to the nuclear threat. Death Studies, 12, 227-251.

The preparation of this essay involved many references. The complete reference listing is available from the author.

Looking Ahead:
National & Global Action for Families

M. Janice Hogan

M. Janice Hogan, Ph.D.
Professor of Family Social
Sciences
University of Minnesota

"The ultimate goal is for family professionals to think and act as part of the global village, to collaborate with professionals cross-nationally, and to work together on a local, national, and global agenda for families."

The United Nations challenges the leaders of countries to give renewed attention to families. The world of families that we all share is dynamic, complex, evolving and important in the fabric of daily life. We are concerned that changes in families and their environment reduce the ability of families to effectively care for their members and to meet other goals. Policy makers, educators, researchers, and practitioners need to share their knowledge and concerns with families and to form a partnership with them. We need to work together cooperatively on a local, national, and global agenda for families.

POSSIBLE, PROBABLE AND PREFERABLE FAMILY FUTURES

In looking ahead, what are the possible, the probable and the preferable futures for families? Is it possible for more families to experience nurturing relationships, adequate resources, healthy outcomes for children, equitable gender roles, and interdependent living across the generations? Anything is possible given the right circumstances, adequate resources and a collaborative spirit. Possibilities and probabilities for families are different concepts. The rates of marriage, cohabitation, fertility, divorce, remarriage, abuse, poverty, and chemical dependency enable us to project the probability of positive and negative family changes over the life cycle and into the future. Our challenge is to design new prevention and intervention strategies aimed at increasing the probability of greater positive experiences in families.

While families vary in describing their preferred future, most will agree with the United Nations' symbol for the Year of the Family[1]. The symbol is a heart sheltered by a roof, linked to a smaller heart representing life, love, warmth, caring, security, togetherness, tolerance and acceptance. The brush stroke open design represents its connection to society and continuity--with a hint of uncertainty. I would add to the analysis of the United Nations' symbol that families are active, dynamic agents of change. They participate in important changes and exchanges in their community, and in designing the future, need to be more proactive. Families can be assisted in their roles by the collaborative energies of political, economic, cultural, religious and legal systems.

PAST LINKED TO FUTURE

Looking ahead involves connecting with the past, remembering that families have always been complex, evolving, and dynamic. The myth that families were stronger, happier, and healthier in earlier decades and centuries has been challenged by family historians. Families have always struggled with relationship, resource and human development issues throughout history. There never was a universal, ideal, traditional family. It may be more enlightening to conceptualize the evolution of families within a dynamic environment and appreciate the diversity of families that live together on this planet.

Over time and across countries, the resiliency of families has been repeatedly tested. Some persistent problems that have challenged society include relationship, resource and human development issues. More specifically, they are issues of gender equity, family violence, racism, ethnic and religious prejudice, fertility and birth circumstances, and resource adequacy problems. In addition, over time and across countries families have experienced crises created by critical illnesses, disabilities, accidents, death, divorce, desertion, criminal assault, unemployment, civil unrest and war, economic depression, natural disasters, and other stressors. Implicit in most of these family problems are external and internal factors--politics, economics, cultural beliefs and customs, and social-psychological dynamics.

ECOLOGICAL MODE

Using an ecological approach is helpful in assessing family issues. It focuses attention on the interaction and exchange between families and other systems. It enables us to recognize the multiple systems with which the family and its members interact. Community service personnel--including many family professionals, legislators, family life educators and family researchers have been challenged to understand the web of systems external to the family and their roles in supporting families. For example, many families with resource-needs issues receive economic assistance from kin since families are the major source of welfare. In addition, government assistance, community services, church outreach and other programs may provide resources, often aimed at meeting only survival needs. As the global economy changes its labor needs, some families face serious economic stressors, a trend that is likely to continue. This is a special concern to families who experience racial, ethnic, and religious prejudice and discrimination--a major injustice which desperately needs solutions in many nations. It is important for countries to examine the impact of their economic policies on families' well-being and to compare the outcomes with policies in other countries. Researchers are critical partners in an important national and global action agenda for the evaluation and redesign of service and benefit programs from government, communities, and private systems.

The level of complexity of family problems leads many specialized groups of professionals to develop partnership projects, e.g., family-community research, treatment programs-family research. Some funding agencies have been giving preference to collaborative projects, based on the premise that they are more comprehensive and more effective. Mattessich and Monsey (1992) reviewed research on collaboration in the areas of social science, health, education and public affairs. They identified six major factors that influence the success of collaborative projects. Briefly, they are: (1) environment such as a history of cooperation and the political-social climate, (2) members characteristics--mutual respect and trust of collaborators, and a team representing a cross-section of those affected, (3) process and structure--collaborators share a stake in process, and the hierarchy is involved, (4) open and frequent, formal and informal communication, (5) a concrete, unique, and attainable purpose and a shared vision, and (6) adequate resources, including the financial means and the skills of the convener. Member characteristics proved to be a vital factor in most of the studies. They concluded that collaboration is powerful, yet a fragile process.

Exemplary Action on Behalf of Families

INTERNATIONAL COLLABORATION

The international community of family professionals needs to strengthen collaboration efforts. Curriculum, research, policy, and practice can be greatly enhanced by looking beyond our national borders. The expanded opportunities through new communication technology to access and generate new knowledge cross-nationally are primary reasons for increased global action. Our common concerns mandate action. Also, the desire to know the world and its families is a powerful force for international collaboration. Several examples of collaborative projects provide ideas for successful models.

A directory of programs, consultants and resource materials, Strengthening Families Through International Innovations Transfer (1992), was developed by the

National Association of Social Workers with a grant from the U.S. Department of
Health and Human Services. They have facilitated the publication of an international
exchange of exemplary models for effective family support. For example, they describe
the Cirkus Solskin program in Denmark which provides for at-risk youth and elderly
individuals to work and learn together. Other programs are from Israel, India, Pakistan,
Kenya, Zambia, Hong Kong, Philippines, Venezuela, Brazil, England, Canada, and the
United States. Each program description includes goals, philosophy, history, services,
results, and staffing.

The Healthy Cities Project which focuses on teenage pregnancy rates, maternal
mortality, and women's health issues in Vienna, Glasgow, St. Petersburg, Gothenburg,
and Clark County, Indiana recognizes that the family-community interdependency in
health is a global issue (Flynn & Dennis, 1993). These international collaborators are
examining the participation of local leaders in improving supportive environments for
families. The underlying rationale for this cross-national project is to better understand
the cultural, political, economic, and legal context of family well-being.

One of the challenges of working cross-nationally is the lack of agreement on the
definition of family. In working with Russian family scholars since 1988 on a collaborative book (Maddock, Hogan, Antonov & Matskovsky, 1993), we discovered in our
first working session that we used different definitions of the family. The Russian
scholars excluded married couples without children in their definition of family and did
not recognize cohabiting couples. And, homosexuality was invisible and illegal
(homosexuality has since gained legal status in Russia). Later, in working with members of the Russian Parliament during 1992 and 1993--prior to their dismissal by
President Boris Yeltsin on September 21, 1993, I learned that the Parliamentary
Committee[2] working on family issues was proposing a broader family definition. It
included all legal and defacto (cohabitation) marriages. One of the factors supporting
this change was what they had learned from research surveys that about two million
more Russian women than men reported being married. This change in definition is not
just a cultural change; it determines those families which are eligible for subsidies.
Thus, the proposed definition is also a political, legal, and economic change.

Hanks and Sussman (1993) recognized that in cross-national research, efforts to
understand the family should take priority over attempts to define the family. Citing the
Cross-National Research Studies on the Family Project which was initiated in 1968,
they describe the fluid definition of family that allowed researchers from ten countries
to incorporate societal variations into their data analysis and interpretation. They
remind us that conceptual consensus in the definition of family may not be appropriate
or possible because of cultural differences. Rather, they urge conceptual clarity where
the working team members have a clear understanding of the cultural variations.

Hanks and Sussman identify the essentials for success of a cross-national scholarly
project as adequate staff and funding, group cohesion, knowledge of the human
condition in all countries involved, in-service education and continuous training, and
contractual agreements. Commitment and passion, complementary skills, and interdependency of the team are also discussed as important for collaborative research and
publication projects.

Finally, members of the National Council on Family Relations (NCFR) developed
initiatives for the United Nations International Year of the Family. Our goals are: (1) to
promote international and multicultural understanding of families through informed
dialogue and through the use of resources such as international bibliographic and
empirical databases, (2) to encourage the development of research agendas sensitive to
multicultural variability, and the use of theories that promote recognition of variability
in families, (3) to infuse curricula, programs, and policies with the richness of understanding families that can only be gained from international and multicultural perspec-

tives, and (4) to build an enriched understanding of the variability of families into the design of educational programs, intervention programs, and the process of marriage and family therapy.

A number of activities, programs, and events are being implemented by NCFR members. This book, One World, Many Families, is intended to expand the international dialogue on family issues and to provoke thoughtful, informed discussion of policies, programs, and practices. A forum to discuss global comparisons regarding health care programs and policies will focus attention on family health issues.[3] "Families and Justice: From Neighborhoods to Nations," is the theme of the 1994 NCFR Annual Conference. And, NCFR members from many nations--Sweden, Israel, Australia, Canada, Belgium, and the United States, planned a summer workshop, "The Future of Families: Mandate for New Initiatives."[4]

The workshop participants are challenged to search the globe for potential solutions to family issues--before, during, and after the workshop. They will bring a proposal, a model initiative or resource materials to the workshop for members of their task force. Each task force will focus on one of seventeen family issues: family peace, substance abuse, divorce, family economics, poverty, immigrant and refugee families, religion, sexuality, child care, marriage and intimate relationships, fertility and circumstances of birth, aging in the family system, health, family law and rights, ethnicity and racial diversity, gender roles and family work, and family violence. Resources such as international bibliographic and empirical data bases will be explored and shared. NCFR will publish the initiatives in public policy, research, education, and practice proposed by each of the task forces. The opportunity to network with experienced family professionals from different parts of the globe and work on the action agenda for families should lead to long term collaboration.

Looking Ahead

We are privileged with a great collective wisdom among the family professionals which can be harnessed to strengthen families globally. While thinking globally and ecologically are not new ideas for educators, researchers, therapists, family advocates, and policy analysts, acting as a global village is new. Our community and national problems can now be traced to issues confronting the global family. When we find ourselves without effective solutions for the family issues at home, we can look to the thousands of naturally evolving experiments in other homes and communities across the planet to consider alternatives. The global village offers many opportunities for generating new knowledge, not only about families in other countries, but also of ourselves and our communities. It sharpens our vision. The ultimate goal is for family professionals to think and act as part of the global village, to collaborate with professionals cross-nationally, and to work together on a local, national, and to work together on a local, national, and global agenda for families.

References

Flynn, B. C. & Dennis, L. I. (1993). Healthy families in healthy cities: A global responsibility. In K. Altergott (Ed.) One World, Many Families. Minneapolis, MN: National Council on Family Relations, 32-37.

Hanks, R. S. & Sussman, M. B. (1993) Clarifying family and its social context: An issue in cross-national research. Proceedings of the XXIII Theory Construction and

Research Methodology Workshop, National Council on Family Relations Annual Conference, November 10-11, Baltimore, Maryland, 135-146.

Maddock, J. W., Hogan, M. J., Antonov, A. I. & Matskovsky, M. S. (1993). Families before and after perestroika: Russian and U.S. perspectives. New York: Guilford.

Mattessich, P. W. & Monsey, B. R. (1992). Collaboration: What makes it work. St. Paul, MN: Amherst H. Wilder Foundation.

Strengthening families through international innovations transfer: A directory of programs, consultants, and resource materials. (1992) Washington, DC: National Association of Social Workers.

Sussman, M. & Hanks, R. (1993). Clarifying family: An issue for cross-national research. Paper delivered at the National Council on Family Relations National Conference, November 10, 1993.

Endnotes

[1] See 1994 International Year of the Family: The Official Emblem and Its Use, United Nations, 1991, p.1.

[2] In a meeting with the Russian parliament Committee for Women, Protection of the Family, Maternity, and Childhood, March 16, 1992, the Deputies talked about the proposed new law which included defacto marriage (cohabitation) and the inclusion of illegitimate children in subsidies to families. The following year when four members of the Russian Parliament Committee were in Minnesota, they described the difficulty of getting any family policy passed by the parliament.

[3] The International Health Policy Forum features Stephen Lewis, UNICEF, Julia Walsh, M.D., Harvard University, and Cynthia Myntti, Humphrey Institute on Public Affairs, University of Minnesota (formerly with the Ford Foundation, Jakarta, Indonesia). It was held November 13, 1993, at the NCFR Annual Conference, Baltimore, MD and is available on audio and video tape from the NCFR Office.

[4] The workshop will be held July 29-August 1, 1994, in Black Mountain, NC. For additional information, contact the National Council on Family Relations office, 3989 Central Avenue NE, Suite 550, Minneapolis, MN 55421 USA.